SONG OF ANGELS

VOLUME I:
EXPERIENCING THE ATMOSPHERE OF HEAVEN

FREDDY HAYLER

Have you ever gazed out the window of an airplane into a sea of clouds, or lay on your back in the grass on a lazy summer afternoon watching the clouds float by? If there were music in those clouds, how would it sound? Freddy Hayler offers us a taste of that aerial symphony. Brilliantly combining majestic melodies that stir the soul with lyrics that stir the spirit, *Song of Angels®* takes the listener on a journey to the heavenlies. Relax, picture that lazy summer afternoon, and listen to and read the *Song of Angels®*.

—Bob Weiner, Evangelist
Youth Now Ministries

I love to listen to his music and hear his message and be there when he worships in his own inimitable style.

—Tommy Tenney, Evangelist
Author of *The God Chasers*

A fresh, new sound of heaven with a powerful, prophetic message best describes this new project entitled *Song of Angels®*. True worship was never intended to be an entertainment media, but was intended to be an outward expression of a deep, inward love for our creator God. Freddy Hayler's album and book are on the cutting edge of the era leading us back to true worship and holiness. Experience God's presence through this refreshing, new sound of God's prophetic voice in this new hour of "Golden Altar" worship.

—Dick Reuben, Evangelist
Sound of the Shofar Ministries
Teacher and leader, Brownsville Revival

Are we sincerely hungry for a genuine visitation from God? Are we truly willing to pursue the Lord regardless of the cost? The music and message of Freddy Hayler help to issue a clarion call for this nation. My friend, we must cry out to God in heartfelt repentance. His ears are waiting to hear our humble pleas for mercy. His eyes are longing to behold us on bended knee. The only hope for our nation is true Holy Ghost revival. God will do His part; we must be willing to do ours.

—Stephen L. Hill, Evangelist
Awake America Ministries

Editorial note: Even at the cost of violating grammatical rules, we have chosen not to capitalize the name satan and related names.

Front cover art ©2001 Golden Altar Records, Inc.

SONG OF ANGELS©

ISBN-13: 978-0-88368-664-5
ISBN: 0-88368-664-3
Printed in the United States of America
©2001 by Freddy Hayler

Whitaker House
1030 Hunt Valley Circle
New Kensington, PA 15068
www.whitakerhouse.com

2 3 4 5 6 7 8 9 10 11 12 13 / 14 13 12 10 09 08 07 06

NO. 1

Song of Angels®

Experience the atmosphere of heaven!

s the church of Jesus Christ enters the new millennium, it has been my fervent desire before God to sing and share a prophetic word fresh from the heart of the Lord that is much needed for the body of Jesus Christ at this hour. God is now birthing a *reformation* and holiness revival movement of supernatural power that is spreading throughout the earth, and I believe that He is giving us new songs and lyrics in these days to correspond with this movement. God is raising up consecrated vessels with a standard of holiness for this end-times reformation music. "The Spirit of Elijah" has indeed come upon the church in this final hour to purify and to separate the holy from the profane, the wheat from the tares, the clean from the unclean, the true from the false, the sheep from the goats, and to discern between good and evil. After all, division is not always a bad thing. God divided the light from the darkness. He loves things that are pure. The spirit of holiness will always come to consecrate and separate God's people unto Himself (Matthew 3:1–12; 13:38–49; 25:31–34; Hebrews 5:14). God is preparing for Himself a bride without spot or wrinkle (Ephesians 5:27)!

To receive vision and fresh biblical messages from the heart of God and to combine them with beautiful derivative melodies is a great privilege. A "new song" and "new sound" are needed for those believers who are earnestly seeking God's love, holiness, and presence to fill their lives. People today in the body of Christ worldwide are thirsting for the tangible presence of God in the music they listen to and the worship they participate in. In this modern generation of believers, we should more than ever want God to be pleased with the song of our hearts. The prophet Amos said, concerning the church music of his day, *"Take away from Me the noise of your songs, for I will not hear the melody of your stringed instruments. But let justice run down like water, and righteousness like a mighty stream"* (Amos 5:23–24 NKJV).

You see, like the prophet Amos, we must understand that the message of the *Song of Angels®* is not just about the manner in which we sing to Jesus, whether in church or in our private time. It is not even about the "sound" or ethereal quality and rapturous, sonorous way in which God's wonderful angels sing in heaven! In fact, the *Song of Angels®* is a clarion call for God's people to enter the fullness of His presence in their praise and worship. Jesus is saying that if we'll get hungry for Him, He will get close to us. Our own brokenness before God is what creates openness in the heavens. But passion and hunger for God are not enough! God desires pure, crystal clear, transparent souls, free of moral impurity and consumed with His holy, fiery presence.

Song of Angels® is, in fact, a final call for the righteous remnant of Joseph (who fled from sin) to model to the world a living, pure, Levitical worship with holy lifestyle and service. This is the hour of reformation, and God is preparing His people to join the angelic, heavenly hosts in the "general song."

> **"Today there is such a noise coming up before the throne of the Most High—the clamor of so-called praise, singing, and joyful shouting. But I wonder if the same people...really have such an intense glory in their secret life with the Lord....Do you still have the same passionate joy in your spirit, just to be alone with the living God?"**
>
> **—Keith Green**

Therefore, in these last days, God is looking for transparent souls and transparent music full of His purity, holiness, peace, and righteousness.

The Message
Celestial encounters of divine hope!

The *Song of Angels*® is a message of hope! Jesus, the Holy Spirit, and God's angels desire for you to know that they will literally move heaven and earth to restore, heal, and save anyone who will call upon Christ with a childlike heart. If you have a broken life, God wants you to come to Him so that He can fix it. In fact, God wants us to know that angels have been sent to minister and encourage all believers in Christ Jesus (Hebrews 1:14)!

The Father's Love

As a youth in Williamsburg, Virginia, I remember hearing Corrie ten Boom (of the movie, *The Hiding Place*)

preach the most powerful sermon I've ever heard. She told many stories that night, but one that stands out the most is the story she told about her godly father, "Papa" ten Boom. One day when she was a very young child playing with her favorite toy, she broke it. It was so satisfying for her to know she could run to her loving father and say, "Papa, could you please fix this?" She went on to teach the principle that if a loving, earthly father would not hesitate for a moment to fix his child's toy if it was within his power to do so, so it is with our heavenly Father. If something is broken in our lives, He longs to fix it. He gave His only Son to save us from our sins. He sent the Holy Spirit to give us peace and joy in this world, and He created the angels to fulfill His Word and to minister to the heirs of salvation (Hebrews 1:7, 14). If you have a broken life today (maybe you've lost a loved one, have a problem with your marriage or family, are anxious or depressed, have inordinate fear or problems with your finances, have a child who is wayward, or have some life-threatening disease, or something similar), simply go to your heavenly Father and say, "Papa, please fix this." And you know what? God will! God will turn your "mess" into a miracle. Seek Him with all your heart (Jeremiah 29:13; 33:3)! As you come to Him with childlike faith, calling upon His name, He will minister His life and breath, His peace and joy, His mercy and love, His tranquility and acceptance into your life. God wants you to know that He longs to fellowship with you and that the "song" in the *Song of Angels®* is Jesus, the joy of all creation! Yes, in His presence is salvation and fullness of joy!

My Prayer

I pray, as you listen to the album and read this book, that you are supernaturally enveloped by and embraced in God's love—healed in spirit, soul, and body by God's sweet anointing and brought into the refining fires of His presence. I pray that your spirit may soar into the heavenlies to see the stones of fire, the throne of God, and the One from whom all love, order, and peace emanate to the entire universe. Yes, He's the God who can fix anything in your life! God has always answered fervent prayer (James 5:14–16). Our God is a God of hope, not a God of despair. He is the God of the impossible (Matthew 19:26)! Jesus said, *"Have faith in God"* (Mark 11:22). In the original Greek, that means to have the faith *of* God. *"Whosoever shall say unto this mountain* [whether it be a "mountain" of spiritual, physical, mental, financial, or marital trouble], *Be thou removed, and be thou cast into the sea; and shall not doubt in his heart, but shall believe that those things which he sayeth shall come to pass; he shall have whatsoever he saith. There-*

fore I say unto you, What things soever you desire, when ye pray, believe that ye receive them, and ye shall have them. And when ye stand praying, forgive" (Mark 11:23–25).

> "Faith sees the invisible, believes the unbelieveable, and receives the impossible."
> —Corrie ten Boom,
> Williamsburg Lodge, 1976

> "We never test the resources of God until we attempt the impossible."
> —F. B. Meyer

"With God nothing shall be impossible" (Luke 1:37).

We as Christians must not become bitter or unforgiving because of some of the hypocrisies evident in the church today. We must not let the poison of a critical, censorious spirit rob us of our love, joy, peace, and kindness (Ephesians 4:31–32). This snare of unforgiveness will cause us to lose the capacity to be used by God in this final hour. The love of many in the last days has indeed waxed cold because of bitterness (Matthew 24:12). We must not let our love grow cold in these days. We need to allow God to fill our homes with His loving, gentle presence and fill the atmosphere of our households with joyous praise and pure worship. The songs of the *Song of Angels*® endeavor to take you into a new place in the heavenlies—to acquire a taste for the glory of God, and to relate to a future home in God.

The God of Future Hope

When Abraham's wife was too old in the natural to give birth to the child of promise, God told Abraham, "Your Isaac is coming!" Later, God caused Sarah to give birth to Isaac, whose seed would be as numerous as the stars of the night sky. In another case, when the widow woman lost her only son, God sent Elijah to raise him from the dead. The spirit of Elijah is here and present today to raise you up and to heal you this very hour! When everyone around Jarius mourned and wept for the loss of his young daughter, Jesus pushed through the hopelessness and despair and raised her from the dead. What great joy was in that home!

Serious Angels

But there was also another message the Lord wanted me to share with you from this vision—things that will challenge all of us to become more Christlike. (I do not claim to have arrived!) For the hour is short, and the message that I heard is a very sobering one. Many times in the Bible, God is mentioned as a God of fire. (See Deuteronomy 4:24; Psalm 97:3; Malachi 3:2; Revelation 1:14.) He is also mentioned as the God of lightning and thunders! (See Exodus 19:16; 20:18; Revelation 4:5.) Today, more than ever, we truly need to have a healthy fear of God in order to understand all aspects of His nature.

Divine Perception

We also need, more than ever, to discern between good and evil (see Hebrews 5:14; Romans 16:19; 1 Corinthians 2:14–16), for that is our defense! Remember, Lot lost most of his family to the destruction of God's wrath because, as the head of his house, he allowed his lukewarm family to develop a refined taste for the evil offered by the predominant culture of the "cosmopolitan" cities Sodom and Gomorrah (Luke 17:29; 2 Peter 2:6)! God wants to show us the way to the abundant life and deliver us from idols that produce no life or peace in us.

God Loves Purity!

True Levitical singers, as with the priests of Bible times, will keep themselves pure from public and private habitual sin in order for God's anointing to flow through them. They will be true worshippers of God, and men and women of prayer and purity.

"Who shall ascend into the hill of the LORD? or who will stand in his holy place? He that hath clean hands, and a pure heart….This is the generation of them that seek him, that seek thy face" (Psalm 24:3–4, 6).

We need a baptism of clear seeing. We need people with prophetic vision. Elijah on Mount Carmel not only prayed, but his eyes were kept open to see the rising cloud. The prophet Ezekiel could foresee a generation of false ministers and singers who, like the proverbial pied piper, would lead God's people away from the straight and narrow way of holiness and salvation.

"So they come to you as people do, they sit before you as My people, and they hear your words, but they do not do them; for with their mouth they show much love, but their hearts pursue their own gain. Indeed you are to them a very lovely song of one who has a pleasant voice and can play well on an instrument; for they hear your words, but they do not do them" (Ezekiel 33:31–32 NKJV).

God is looking for true worshippers (John 4:23–24)! God is seeking lives that are a living and holy sacrifice acceptable to Him (Romans 12:1–2). God is grieved by the popular message of "easy believism" and the doctrine of cheap grace. Yet I believe that today is a new day, and God is raising up a generation of end-times, sincere Christian believers and warriors who will, in fact, "live the life." Any true and lasting revival will be built upon the spiritual bedrock of repentance, prayer, fasting, and holiness. A famous revivalist has said, "The *depth* of your repentance will determine the *height* of your revival!"

The Final Generation

I believe that *we* are the generation that will seek His face earnestly. God is tired of being second place to everything else in our lives. He wants us to dwell in His presence. God wants us to see and touch His glory. God wants fellowship and intimacy. He wants us to know Him in a deeper realm. His desire for us is to live and be holy as He is holy (1 Peter 1:16; Hebrews 12:14). We need an outpouring of the fresh, manifest presence of the Almighty. God's end-times reformation people will, after a busy day at work, *run* to the prayer closet and seek Christ in private or with their spouses. May the Lord deliver us from dead orthodoxy! God desires us to have a vision and impartation of His holy nature even as the ancient prophet Isaiah (Isaiah 6:1–6)!

The Burning Bush
Divine perception: Guidance in the glory

It is spiritually impossible to truly trust in God while there is habitual failure to wait upon Him for guidance and direction. Your hunger will determine your future. Therefore, a reformation people needs, more than ever, guidance and spiritual discernment in this hour. (See Ecclesiastes 8:5; Luke 12:56; 1 Corinthians 2:14; Hebrews 5:14.) God will provide it! Yet we must understand that God is searching for hearts into which He can pour His presence. The question is, Are you hungry for His presence? Again, your hunger will determine your life destiny in Christ, for in God's presence you will find His will, and you will be made holy.

The burning bush refers to specific revelation and direction for God's will to be accomplished in your life. The burning bush was the means by which God spoke to Moses His specific will and plan to deliver His people from the bondage and captivity of Egypt. Do you want a burning bush? Do you want direction for your life, your family, your job, your ministry? You need to get before a burning bush; that is, get into the fire of God, get in the glory through prayer (Exodus 24:9–18). You need a burning bush experience.

Moses, our example, after worshipping God and getting a vision from God, had a heart that was enlarged enough to see a pattern of ministry from God! It was after that glorious vision and many other magnificent encounters with God on mountaintops that Moses received the instructions to build the tabernacle—an eternal paradigm for the worship of God. From this pattern, we Christians today know that the way to God's holiest place is through the brazen altar of Christ's sacrifice, the outer courts of praise, the inner court of worship, and on into the holiest place of God's divine presence and glory. Peter's, James', and John's hearts were enlarged while seeing Jesus in His glorified form on the Mount of Transfiguration (Matthew 17:1–8). God was preparing them in their ministries for what was to come next by giving them a vision of His glory.

Knowing Christ Intimately

Do you know Him in His glory? Do you know Him as Savior, Healer, Provider? Do you know Him as the King of Glory (Psalm 24:7–10)? Are you thrilled at the sound of His voice? Do you worship Him enough in intimacy to smell His very fragrance? Are you praying for a burning bush experience? Can you truly say you are flowing in His fresh oil, or is the oil within you stale and rancid? God is here right now to embrace you, to still your storm, to cause your

troubles to cease, and to fill you with new oil.

Come Away, My Beloved

> **"The branch of the vine does not worry, and toil, and rush here to seek for sunshine, and there to find rain. No, it rests in union and communion with the vine. Let us so abide in the Lord Jesus."**
> **—James Hudson Taylor**

God is calling you to abide with Him in intimate prayer, for all true holiness is rooted in prayerful repose in Christ. God is present right now to show you His heart—to set your heart ablaze with His glory and His love! Do you hear the angels sing when you worship? Do you go into the glory beyond the veil? God has anointed you and appointed you to worship! Don't let the devil or your negative thinking persuade you that even your simplest prayers and sincere worship are not sweet incense to the King of Glory! Come away into the glory realm with your Beloved, into the realm of eternity, and taste of His manifest presence! Let God manifest His glory through you to reach others on earth. Do not think that you are unable to sing and worship unto the Lord, for God finds much pleasure in your songs to Him.

Do not say in your heart, "I'll never be able to sing or hear the Song of Angels®." *"God is no respecter of persons"* (Acts 10:34). During the Great Reformation, John Wesley and thirteen hundred other believers heard a little of the Song of Angels®. From Wesley's diary we gather the following experience: "Being Good Friday, I came to Mansfield, to assist in the services that day. While we were ministering the sacrament to about thirteen hundred people, I heard a low, soft, solemn tone, just like that of an Aeolian harp. It continued five or six minutes, and so affected many that they could not refrain from tears. It then gradually faded away."

If we could but catch one strain of heaven's pure melody, it would spoil us from earthly sounds forever! We must begin to see things from heaven's side, where all is love, joy, and peace. It is my prayer that, after hearing this album and reading this book, God would give you the desire to hear His heavenly sounds, for God is a rewarder of those who diligently seek Him (Hebrews 11:6).

A Prophecy to You

Thus saith the Lord...

"As you enter My holy place, as you pass the brazen altar, as you pass the priest who sings My prayer and who burns sweet incense to Me, quietly come into the Holy Place, and sit at My feet, oh, My beloved child. How I long to hold you close, so close to Me, that I may anoint you to work for Me. Come closer to Me and feel the heart-beat of My love for you. Feel the dew of the angels, and listen to the soft flutter of angel wings, for it is in that place that I will sweetly whisper to you secrets of My glory. Come, for I give you fresh oil now. I am pouring it upon your head to loose you from the bands of oppression. Come, send up your prayers. Kneel in My glory. Send up your worship. What loving father or mother does not love and cherish the voice of his or her child? Even the newborn baby talk is lovely to Me! I find great pleasure in your worship, child of the Most High God. Stand guard for My presence, and I will show you My secrets. Shhhhhh…. Come closer and be quiet. Listen to My still, small voice. Let My love flow into all the deep places and hurts in your heart. Worship your Beloved in all intimacy (Song of Solomon 2:8; 4:9–15), for I am the fairest of ten thousand. Hush, My child. May all your storms be stilled. *'Peace, be still'*

(Mark 4:39)."

The Glory for Our Defense

The glory of His presence is our shield and first line of defense against the attacks of satan. Whenever the people of Israel worshiped, they had the victory, and so should we! (See 2 Chronicles 20:21–22.)

"And the LORD will create upon every dwelling place of mount Zion, and upon her assemblies, a cloud and smoke by day, and the shining of a flaming fire by night: for upon all the glory shall be a defense" (Isaiah 4:5).

God wants you to enter His rest (Exodus 33:12–14; Hebrews 4:9–10). He wants us, like the heavenly-minded Jacob, to climb the ladder of His glory, ascend into the heavens into His throne room, and sit at His feet. God will bring us into a place of His refreshing in the glory. In His presence is joy forevermore! In His presence in glory, there is no want of guidance, direction, discernment, or perception.

Holy Vision

It is my prayer that the anointing of God upon the music from *Song of Angels*® will assist you in coming into the presence of a mighty, majestic, holy Creator. I pray that the message will cause you to examine your heart. Let God search your heart entirely so that you will desire to repent, pray, fast, and seek His face more earnestly. *The time of His coming is at hand!* There is a sense of divine urgency among God's prophets in the earth. God is looking carefully at heart motives and is coming for a bride *"not having spot or wrinkle…holy and without blemish"* (Ephesians 5:27).

Father of Lights

It is also my hope that this compila-

© 2001 M. Dudash

NO. 5

tion of timeless, sacred songs called *Song of Angels®*, as well as this small book, will inspire your "inner man" to look up into the brilliant, glowing face of Jesus; to see the myriads of angels and heavenly hosts worshipping before His throne; to come and fly upward into the sparks and lightnings of His glorious presence; yes, even to see your soul's true eternal destiny! It has been said that the true character of the Christian has little to do with the public life as much as how one lives before God *privately.* Therefore, let us earnestly seek God's face in private. For wherever God directs His face there is great favor; there is forgiveness, salvation, divine health, deliverance, healing, grace, prosperity, peace, joy, majesty, and abundance! I pray that each listener will get a foretaste of heavenly vision and join with all the heavenly hosts in adoration to Jesus Christ—the joy of all creation! The church of the Lord Jesus Christ is worthy of the finest music that human hearts, through the power of the Holy Spirit, can be inspired to create. For all true and lasting gifts come down from the *"Father of lights"* (James 1:17).

Declare His Glory

In the final reformation, the church's old patterns of theological learning, religious pride, human wisdom, and wrong religious mentalities will be swept aside by a powerful, fresh outpouring of God's Spirit. A reformation people will learn not to exalt any man or woman, personality, church, or denomination, but will glorify Jesus and His person alone!

Man may not take credit for anything that God Almighty has given. He will share His glory with no one. But one day in heaven, He will willingly share it with those who truly live for Him in this world. If there's anything good or beautiful, it should all declare His glory! This includes the voice—or any talent that God has given to any individual.

God Loves You!

God the Father loves you. Jesus loves you. The Holy Spirit loves you! Therefore, as you open your heart while listening to this music, any "goose bumps" feeling you may experience is, in fact, the glorious, physical presence of the Holy Spirit hovering over you with His love. Each song was sung only after much prayer and only after the anointing of God was upon the singer. Again, it is important to note that God requires the same rites of consecration for singers and sacred musicians as He does for His priests (Ezra 2:40–41, 70; 7:24). Why do Christian singers and musicians think even for a moment that they need not fast, pray, and live purely, even as a pastor or evangelist must live? Anything less is a "mixture," which God hates. (See Ezekiel 33:31–32; Matthew 7:15–17; Luke 6:43–49; Romans 12:1–10; 1 Peter 3:3–4; 1 John 2:15–17.)

Jesus' Burden Is Light!

There are many distractions in our high-tech lifestyle and fast-paced society (unlike the experience of the ancients) that will become weights to our lives. Satan will attempt to burden God's people with anxiety, strife, frustration, and even depression. God tells us to lay these things aside (Hebrews 12:1).

Jesus said, "*Come unto me, all ye that labour and are heavy laden, and I will give you rest. Take my yoke upon you, and learn of me; for I am meek and lowly in heart: and ye shall find rest unto your souls. For my yoke is easy, and my burden is light*" (Matthew 11:28–30). Religious legalism as a means to holiness is a killer that will rob you of joy. However, loving Christ and living

NO. 4

prayerfully in His presence is the way to receive His holiness with peace and joy. Holiness, therefore, is birthed out of relationship with Jesus. Thus, we should love His moral laws because they are intrinsically good and emanate from God's own nature. They are *"light"* and *"easy"* on the soul that He has created. Your constitution as His creature was not created to handle the "wear and tear" of sin.

"Grace abuse" winks at sin and trifles with the devil. Living in a state of grace abuse is a dangerous pastime. Be not deceived; there is no liberty or peace living in sin or worldliness. The devil's insurance company never pays its claims. A false kind of unconverting faith is one to avoid at all costs (James 2:19–20)! Obeying Jesus and abiding in Him is your best insurance policy.

It is satan and sin that bring a heavy burden—bondage to guilt, depression, lust, addictions, and so on. This is what makes life hard! It's the devil's yoke that is heavy, not God's law of liberty. God's law is liberating to the soul. We have joy in obeying God's moral laws, because we are designed to be holy as He is! The design of your soul by the Master Jesus was never meant to bear the weight of sin. Therefore, abide in the wonderful, loving presence of Jesus moment by moment every day of your life, and let the fruit of His Holy Spirit bring forth joy, love, and peace in every area of your life—whether in your spiritual life, in your marriage, in your occupation and finances, or in your mind (John 10:10).

True Believers Love God's Law!

Jesus loved God's law, and so should we (Matthew 5:17–19). In Ezra's revival, the whole nation had a celebration over the "rediscovery" of the liberty of God's holy laws (2 Chronicles 5:12, Ezra 6:20–21; 7:7; Nehemiah 12:27–30). The church at that time had a revelation that the law was essentially a transcript of God's own character and nature. Fellowship with God was reestablished on the basis of understanding God's essence and personality and seeking God's holiness. True revival has always been a revival of God's truth and holiness. Has this not been the experience of true church revival throughout history? (Consider, for example, the great Wesley, Whitfield, Finney, and Welsh revivals.) In fact, until we become transparent and pure before God, His glory cannot completely shine through us, so that those masses of souls that dwell in spiritual darkness can see His light and come to the glory of Christ that is emanating forth from our consecrated lives! Let us therefore abide in Him (Isaiah 60:1–3; Matthew 5:14–16).

A Divine Transaction

Therefore, let us now enter into a full *covenant exchange* with Jesus! Let us exchange our filthy garments of sin and pride for His glorious white robes of purity, holiness, and humility. I pray that you are lifted higher and higher into the presence of the third heaven! May the healing waters of the Holy Spirit flow all around you as you listen to the music. My prayer is that many who are imprisoned by habitual sins will find the grace of God to repent and turn to Christ for their salvation; that those who are sick and bound with disease may come and dip in the healing waters of His divine presence. May all of you who thirst and hunger for more of God's tangible anointing be baptized in the fire of His Holy Spirit and in the sweet presence of Jesus, the Lover of your soul! All we must do is love Him and seek Him with all of our hearts (Jeremiah 29:13).

The Mirror of God's Grace

God's grace, by the power of the Holy Spirit, will work Christlikeness in you daily as you yield yourself as an obedient vessel to Him. Your heart will become a reflection back to God the Father of the image of His own dear Son Jesus!

We may live holy lives only through His grace. Defining God's grace simply as "God's unmerited favor" is not sufficient for the Bible meaning of grace. *Grace is power*—power to live a holy life; power to save you *from* your sins, not *in* your sins. I believe a good definition of grace is this:

Grace: God's enabling power working within us by the Holy Spirit, who causes us to be what He has called us to be and to do what He has called us to do; that is, the divine influence of God, the very attributes and "doxa" (glory) of God shining upon our hearts and reflecting upon yielded lives.

This is a more biblical, wholistic view of grace. The Lawgiver Jesus now lives in us, and as we yield to Him and to His sweet Holy Spirit, He will make us holy. This is the great *"mystery"* revealed— *"Christ in you, the hope of glory"* (Colossians 1:27). It is not our ability, but His enabling power working within us to fulfill His will for our lives. So stop striving to be holy; stop living under condemnation; rest in Christ, and let Him live a holy life through you!

Spiritual Immunity

May His holy presence sweetly and gently convict us of all our sins, convince us of His patient, unwavering love, and cause us to abide in His holy presence moment by moment. God wants us to enter a secret place of *spiritual immunity*. But we need to stop watching what we have been watching, stop reading what we have been reading, stop going where we have been going, and get into serious prayer with God and totally surrender to Him.

Jesus Is Coming

The coming of the Majestic One is at hand. Therefore, let us cast aside the sins and weights that have so easily beset us and that have kept us from walking in His glorious presence as in the cool of the day (Hebrews 12:1).

Certainly none of us wants to be ashamed at His coming. God wants you to know this is your day of new beginnings. It doesn't matter how much you've blown it in the past. The Bible says that today is the day of salvation (2 Corinthians 6:2)! I therefore humbly ask you to repent of your sins, forsake your failures, and come to the cross of Christ. Oh, let the powerful, forgiving blood of Jesus cleanse you and keep you from all sin (1 John 1:7, 9)! And after coming to the cross and experiencing Christ's love and forgiveness, it's time to grow up! It's time to ascend into His glory and walk in power so that those in darkness may see His great light in us!

All glory, honor, and power be unto Him, and may His glory (His *"kabod,"* His weightiness, splendor, majesty, and plenteousness) rest upon each of you. Gloria! The message of the *Song of Angels®* is in fact…

Experimentando la atmosfera del cielo (Experience the atmosphere of heaven)!

Adora…hasta que la gloria llegue!

Muevete al ambito de la glorio, y todo se hace posible!

Gloria!

Freddy "Frederico" Hayler

THE MUSIC

Song of Angels® [Song of Michael]

Malise
English Lyrics: Freddy Hayler

"And all of the angels stood round the throne…and the four beasts, and fell before the throne on their faces, and worshiped God" (Revelation 7:11).

"Who maketh his angels spirits, and his ministers a flame of fire….Are they not all ministering spirits, sent forth to minister for them who shall be heirs of salvation?" (Hebrews 1:7, 14).

Freddy Hayler and Rebekah Hayler
(Lyrics in Italian & Spanish)

Io, vorrei	[I desire]
Liberarti	[to liberate you]
Domattina	[at dawn]
E vorrei	[and would like]
Vederti volare	[to see you fly]
Un carro d'angelo	[on chariots of angels]
Al cielo	[on high]
Tu	[you]
El Padre Santo	[with the holy Father]
Espiritu Santo	[with the Holy Spirit]
Angelico	[like an angel]
E l'anima	[and the soul]
Se ne va	[departs]
Verso l'eternita	[to eternity]
Gloria!	[Glory!]

Verse 1
There
In the night sky
Beyond the starlight
In a vision
I see glory
The archangels
And Michael's
Hands raising
Angelic tongues of fire
Flow from his being
God, let me hear
Celestial beauty

**God, help me
Liberate my spirit free
To sing the angels' song
All around Your glorious
throne**

Interlude

The Holy Spirit desires for you to see into the heavenly realms, to see what the angels are doing this moment and what you'll be doing for all eternity before the throne of almighty God. (See Isaiah 6:1–3; Revelation 4:1–6.)

Verse 2

**Lord, help me to see
Your holy face
Illuminated
A blazing beauty
God, help me
Liberate my spirit free
To sing the angels' song
All around Your glorious throne
I hear the angels' song**

"Though I speak with the tongues of… angels" (1 Corinthians 13:1).

from "Rapsodia"
©1994, 2001 Insieme S.r.l./Zucchero & Fornaciari Music S.r.l.
Published in U.S.A. by Sugar-Melodi, Inc.
2001 Song of Angels® Project, Vol. 1

For examples in the Bible of "visions in the night," see Genesis 15:1; 46:2; Numbers 12:6; 1 Samuel 3:1; Proverbs 29:18; Daniel 2:19; 8:16; 10:5-6; 7:7; Joel 2:28; Acts 2:17; 2 Corinthians 12:1.

Mighty God [Gabriel's Chant]
F. Sartori - L. Quarantotto
English Lyrics: Freddy Hayler

"And immediately I was in the spirit: and, behold, a throne was set in heaven, and one sat on the throne. And he that sat was to look upon like a jasper and a sardine stone: and there was a rainbow round about the throne, in sight like unto an emerald. And round about the throne were four and twenty seats: and upon the seats I saw four and twenty elders sitting, clothed in white raiment; and they had on their heads crowns of gold. And out of the throne proceeded lightnings and thunderings and voices: and there were seven lamps of fire burning before the throne, which are the seven Spirits of God. And before the throne there was a sea of glass like unto crystal: and in the midst of the throne, and round about the throne, were four beasts full of eyes before and behind" (Revelation 4:2–6).

"And the twelve gates were twelve pearls; every several gate was of one pearl; and the street of the city was pure gold, as it were transparent glass. And I saw no temple therein: for the Lord God Almighty and the Lamb are the temple of it. And the city had no need of the sun, neither of the moon, to shine in it: for the glory of God did lighten it, and the Lamb is the light thereof" (Revelation 21:21–23).

"And He showed me a pure river of water of life, clear as crystal, proceeding out of the throne of God and of the Lamb" (Revelation 22:1).

"And above the firmament that was over their heads was the likeness of a throne, as the appearance of a sapphire stone: and upon the likeness of the throne was the likeness as the appearance of a man above upon it. And I saw as the colour of amber, as the appearance of fire round *about within it, from the appearance of his loins even upward, and from the appearance of his loins even downward, I saw as it were the appearance of fire, and it had brightness round about. As the appearance of the bow that is in the cloud in the day of rain, so was the appearance of the brightness round about. This was the appearance of the likeness of the glory of the Lord. And when I saw it, I fell upon my face, and I heard a voice of one that spake"* (Ezekiel1:26–28).

I see You now
Shekinah all around You
Adoring angels praise You
Before Your throne
I see glory
Glory in the highest
And an emerald rainbow
Round the throne of God
And a crystal river
Now flowing from Your presence
With Your love and healing
For all the nations

Eyes a liquid flame of love
The holy Lamb shines brighter
Than a billion angels above
And I lift my praise to You
And I will shout for joy
For I have seen His glory
His glory! His glory!

My prayer is for all of you
To know Him
Oh, to really love Him
And to sing God's praises
To worship and to see God's
  glory
Come on and lift your hands high
Like Michael in the sky
And bow down before His holy
  presence
And if you really listen
You'll hear His angel song!

And He'll cause your mind to see
And open the deaf ears
To hear the angels singing to
  Him

And you'll know you're His
And He is yours
And we will shout for joy
For we have touched His glory
Glory!

Interlude
Lift your hands and praise your
  King
And sing and dance for joy
For we have touched the glory
Of a mighty God
Mighty God!

G. Vessicchio - G. Servillo
English Lyrics: Freddy Hayler

"Thou shalt love the LORD *thy God with all thine heart, and with all thy soul, and with all thy might"* (Deuteronomy 6:5).

"I will love thee, O LORD*"* (Psalm 18:1).

God, I love You so
And I pray that You'll be with me
And You'll guide me
Through a world
So very cold
That needs to know
Your great love for them

So when I'm all alone
Upon my bed I dream about
Your lovely face
All I really want is to be closer to
  You, God
And to drink in Your grace

And to hear Your sweet voice
And to be one with God

1st Chorus
O God, I love You so
There's nothing I desire
But Your sweet presence
To feel Your presence now
And see Your glory
All around us
I love You, O God

So dream within your heart
He'll not depart
If you will seek Him
Can you hear Him calling
Through the lattice of the window
In your precious soul
Oh, He is your Beloved
And He'll send His Spirit to you
When you call on Him
With all your heart and mind
And with your strength to cry

2nd Chorus

O God, I love You so
I love You so
I need You, Lord
There's no one else besides my
  Father
There's nothing else
That I, that I desire
I love You, O God

Interlude
So let all bondage go
And feel His healing flow within
  you
Say you love…
Listen to your Savior calling
Say you love Him
And He'll touch you now

From "Sogno"
©1995, 2001 Edizioni Suvini Zerboni S.p.a./
Sugarmusic Edizioni Musicali
S.r.l./Mascotte Edizioni Musicali S.r.l.
Published in U.S.A. by Sugar-Melodi,
Inc.

NO. 6

Spirit of Elijah [Elisha's Song]

English Lyrics: Freddy Hayler
Dedicated to all true prophets who cry out to God for a true revival.

Like Elijah's servant, Elisha, we need the veils removed from our eyes in order to see the spiritual and unseen heavenly hosts who are ministers of fire to those who are the elect of God.

"And it came to pass, as they still went on, and talked, that, behold, there appeared a chariot of fire, and horses of fire, and parted them both asunder; and Elijah went up in a whirlwind to heaven. And Elisha saw it, and he cried, My father, my father....He took up also the mantle of Elijah that fell from him, and went back, and stood by the bank of Jordan" (2 Kings 2:11–13).

"Hear me, O LORD, hear me, that this people may know that thou art the LORD God....Then the fire of the LORD fell, and consumed the burnt sacrifice....And when all the people saw it, they fell on their faces: and they said, The LORD, he is the God; the LORD, he is the God" (1 Kings 18:37–39).

I see amber horses
Ascending in the desert sky
Bright chariots of fire
Burning in a whirlwind
A man is crying
"My father, my father"
As he holds his veil
By the river Jordan

Chorus
Farewell, Elijah
Farewell, my father Elijah
For I lay my mantle down
God, send down the Spirit of Elijah

I hear God's Spirit call
I will surrender all
Sweet Spirit, fall on me
Baptize me in Your fire
And in the glory of

Your presence
Your holy presence
My God and my King

When Jesus showed me
All the lambs not in His fold
And the urgent call to reach
The blind and hurting souls
God of Elijah
Send down the Spirit of Elijah
For I lay my mantle down
Send down the fire of Elijah

I see now a prophet
Who could raise a little boy
And who could calm the cry of
A widow's broken heart
Who will help the Fatherless
Spread true revival in the land
For the filth of baal has destroyed
The minds of common men
For the Spirit of Elijah is the pure
Spirit of the Lord
To empower all those who obey
and will

Pray and seek His holy face
As the dark storm gathers
Let us lay aside our foolish
dreams
And pray like father Abraham to
spare
Our nation from God's wrath

Chorus
God of all power
I hear the voice of the Elijah's call
Consume all evil now
Send down the fire of Elijah
There's just no time around

Prophecy…

Thus says the Lord of Hosts:

"My Spirit will not always strive with man
For the sins of the nations
Have kindled the fire of My wrath
Therefore, My people, humble yourselves
and pray
And repent of your wicked ways

And seek My face, that you may be hid
   in the day of My vengeance
Upon all those that do evil
And despise My law and persecute My
   prophets
But you who walk holy and blameless in
   this hour
You who hear My voice and who know Me
You shall grow strong in the Spirit of Elijah
And shall accomplish great exploits in
   these coming days
For you shall call upon Me for fire
And I will answer you with fire and will send
A true revival to My people
A revival of holiness and power
That will shake the nations
Prepare ye!
Prepare ye!
Prepare ye!

Music: L. Dalla from "Caruso"
Publishing: Ed. BMG Ariola
S.p.a./Assist S.r.l.
Published in U.S.A. by BMG Music
Publishing/EMI Music Publishing 2001

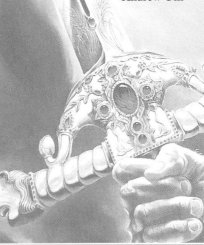

"God's program for reviving His people is definite and clear. First, Elijah repaired the altar of Jehovah that was thrown down. That is the place to begin. All the ruin that sin has wrought must be cleared away by heartfelt repentance and confession. Things must be made right wtih God; restitution must be made where it is due. Unless this is done, definitely and thoroughly, a prayer for revival is vain."

—Andrew Gih

NO. 9

The Call [Abraham's Call]

S. Cirillo - J. Amoruso
English Lyrics: Freddy Hayler

Dedicated to Dr. Costa Dier and International Leadership Seminars, Dr. J. Christy and Betty Wilson, and all who have dedicated their lives to reaching the impoverished and spiritually lost people groups of the world.

"And in thy seed shall all the nations of the earth be blessed; because thou hast obeyed my voice" (Genesis 22:18).

"And he brought him forth abroad, and said, Look now toward heaven, and tell the stars, if thou be able to number them: and he said unto him, So shall thy seed be. And he believed in the LORD; and he counted it to him for righteousness" (Genesis 15:5–6).

**I was sailing home one evening
As I gazed upon the stars**

**And out on the dark horizon
I could count them from afar
They just shined through
The night sky I could see them
   by the thousands**

**And the God who made
Each one of them
And who calls them all by name
Is the same yesterday, today,
   and forever
He has always been the same
As He spoke to Abraham
That His seed could not be
   numbered**

**And I've always wondered
How God could call one godly
   man
And by His loving sovereign
   power
Oh, through him could change
   the destiny of men
For by his faith he overcame
And now his seed's a chosen**

nation
Now you're blessed to be a
   blessing
So all the nations can know
God
Grant me the faith of father
   Abraham
Send me forth to the Gentiles
To a land I do not know
To the souls who wait in
   darkness

Chorus
Lord, we praise You with
   wonder
As we lift our hands to heaven
Our whole hearts now we
   surrender
Oh, to obey Your highest call
Now send us forth to reach
   them all
Send us forth to the nations

[Trumpet Interlude]
Navigando a mi casa a noche

Y miranda las estrellas
En el negro horizonte
Las cuento desde lejos
Brillan en el cielo
Puedo verlas por millares

[Guitar solo]
Oh, to obey Your greatest call
Send us forth to reach them all
To obey the Great Commission

*From "Le Tue Parole"
©1995, 2001 Insieme S.r.l./
Sugarmusic Edizioni
Musicali S.r.l./Double Marpot Edizioni Musicali
Published in U.S.A. by Sugar-Melodi,
Inc.*

Holy Spirit, Please Come

M. Malavasi
English Lyrics: Freddy Hayler

"But ye shall receive power, after that the Holy Ghost is come upon you" (Acts 1:8).

"If ye then, being evil, know how to give good gifts unto your children: how much more shall your heavenly Father give the Holy Spirit to them that ask Him?" (Luke 11:13).

"Who, when they were come down, prayed for them, that they might receive the Holy Ghost" (Acts 8:15).

"Nevertheless I tell you the truth; it is expedient for you that I go away: for if I go not away, the Comforter will not come unto you; but if I depart, I will send him unto you" (John 16:7).

Holy Spirit,
Holy Spirit, please come

Like a spring rain
Fall on me from above
I am thirsty
I am thirsty for Thee
Come and fill me
Comfort me in Your sweet love
Come to me as a gentle dove
Anoint me and release me
To come to Thee
My God and King
Oh, to see Your glory
On the wings of the Dove

Holy Spirit
Jesus said You would come
Like a spring breeze
To breathe life into me
When You fill me
I am happy and calm
As I praise You
I can fly into heaven
How my spirit adores You
To be filled with Your presence
And all I need is Your sweet love
And to see Your glory,

On the wings of the Dove
As I kneel on the floor
I can bear it no more
When the trials of this life
And the tempter is rending
My heart to the core
I lift my hands up
To the heavens
And praise Jesus
For He'll send Him now
On the wings of the Dove

God's pure Spirit of love
For He's conquered all power
Of darkness and fear
And is sent here for you
For me
To help us see our Lord Jesus
Oh, to see Jesus
(Sweet Anointing)
Oh, just to see Your glory
Just to touch Your glory
On the wings of the Dove
The sweet wings of the Dove

[Piano]
Holy Spirit
Jesus said You would come
Like a spring rain
Fall on us from above
Holy Spirit
Please come
Please come

From "Romanza"
©1995,2001Insieme S.r.l./Double
Marpot Edizioni Musicali.
Published in U.S.A. by Sugar-Melodi,
Inc.

NO. 10

Healing Prayer

Rebekah Hayler - Freddy Hayler
New English Lyrics: Freddy Hayler
Italian Lyrics: Alberto Testa - Tony Renis
Music: David Foster - Carol B. Sager

Dedicated to my wife, Annie, and my two lovely daughters, Lindsay and Rebekah, who help me vocally and musically in my concert crusades. Rebekah sang these vocals at ages 11 and 12!

Rebekah - Verse 1

Oh, come, O God, I pray
And touch our lives today
Lord, fill us with Your love
Send healing from above
Let this be our prayer
When we've lost our way
Lead us to a place
Guide us there by faith
Touch and heal us by Your grace

Verse 2 - Duet
Freddy Hayler (Italian lyrics):

La luce che tu dai
Rebekah Hayler (English lyrics):
(I pray you find your Light)
Freddy Hayler:
Nel cuore restero
Rebekah Hayler:
(And hold it in our hearts)
Freddy Hayler:
Ricordarci che
Rebekah Hayler:
(When stars go out each night)
Freddy Hayler:
L'eterna stella sei
Rebekah Hayler:
(O Lord)
Freddy Hayler:
Nella mia preghiera
Rebekah Hayler:
(Let this be our prayer)
Freddy Hayler:
Quanta fede c'e'
Rebekah Hayler:
(When shadows fill our day)
Lead us to a place
Guide us by Your grace

Give us faith so we'll be safe

Chorus
Freddy and Rebekah Hayler:
Sognamo un mondo
Sneza piu violenza
Un mondo di
Giusstizia di speranza
Ognuno dia
La mano al suo vicino
Simbolo di pace
Di Fraternita

Verse 3
Freddy Hayler:
La forza che ci dai
Rebekah Hayler:
(We ask that life be kind)
Freddy Hayler:
E'il desiderio che
Rebekah Hayler:
(Send healing from above)
Freddy Hayler:
O gnuno trovi amor
Rebekah Hayler:
(We hope it's soon we'll find)

Freddy Hayler:
In torno e dentra a se
Rebekah Hayler:
(Deliverance divine)
Freddy Hayler:
Let this be our prayer
Rebekah Hayler:
Let this be our prayer
Freddy Hayler:
Like a little child
Rebekah Hayler:
Like a little child
Freddy and Rebekah Hayler:
Lead us to a place
Guide us by Your grace
Give us faith so we'll be saved
Lift us to a place
Take us there by faith
(A ricorderci che)
(Quanta fede c'e')
Touch and heal us by Your grace

From "The Prayer"
©1998, 2001 Warner-Tamerlane Publishing Corp.
Published in U.S.A. by Warner/Chappell

Healing Waters [Raphael's Song]

E. Morricone - L. Quarantotto
English Lyrics: Freddy Hayler

Dedicated to all sincere healing and evangelistic ministries who minister to the body, soul, and spirit. For thirty-eight years, a man was in physical bondage until Jesus came along one day and touched him with the power of His healing presence.

"For an angel went down at a certain season into the pool, and troubled the water....When Jesus saw him lie, and knew that he had been now a long time in that case, he saith to him, Wilt thou be made whole?" (John 5:4, 6).

"Then he went down, and dipped himself seven times in Jordan, according to the saying of the man of God: and his flesh came again like unto the flesh of a little child, and he was clean [healed]" (2 Kings 5:14).

"Go to the pool of Siloam, and wash: and I went and washed, and I received [healing]" (John 9:11).

"I will make the wilderness a pool of water, and the dry land springs of water" (Isaiah 41:18).

"And God wrought special miracles by the hands of Paul: so that from his body were brought unto the sick handkerchiefs…, and the diseases departed from them, and the evil spirits went out of them" (Acts 19:11–12).

"I am the Lord that healeth thee" (Exodus 15:26).

Verse 1
You waited for so long
By still waters
For the angel to stir the pool
Of healing waters
There's healing for your soul
Our God will make you whole
So please don't despair of life
For even today, my friend,
Jesus will give you life
And He will bear all your pain

To show you how He loves you

1st Chorus
1st Chorus
Lord, stir the healing waters
Cleanse us now
By Your blood
Heal us now
Lord, with Your Word
Come now and touch my mind
And my body
Lord, with Your healing
With Your healing waters

Narrative
Lord Jesus, You are the same
  yesterday, today, and forever
Touch those who hear
Those who would cry out to You
Father, we cry out to You with
  faith
You who raised Lazarus from the
  grave
Who healed a blind man from
  birth
Touch Your people now

Verse 2
There's healing for your soul
Our God will make you whole
So please don't despair of life
For even today, my friend,
Jesus will give you life,
And He'll bear all your pain
To show you how He loves you

2nd Chorus
Lord, stir the healing waters
Feel His healing waters
Now enter the healing river of
  Jesus
For it is flowing
Oh, divine healing waters
Cleanse us now
Heal them now
Touch us now
Healing waters

From "Come Un Fiume Tu"
©1999, 2001 Insieme S.r.l./Almud
Edizioni Musicali S.r.l.
Published in U.S.A. by Sugar-Melodi, Inc.
Orchestration: Mauro Malavasi

The Day the Angels Cried

Music: V. Zelli - M. Mengali - G. Panceri
English Lyrics: Freddy Hayler

"And about the ninth hour Jesus cried with a loud voice, saying, Eli, Eli, lama sabachthani? that is to say, My God, my God, why hast thou forsaken me?" (Matthew 27:46).

"And Jesus said unto him, Verily I say unto thee, To day shalt thou be with me in paradise....And there was a darkness over all the earth until the ninth hour" (Luke 23:43–44).

"And when Jesus had cried with a loud voice, he said, Father, into thy hands I commend my spirit: and having said thus, he gave up the ghost" (Luke 23:46).

He was alone
At the council that night
When all His judges
Falsely accused Him
You may recall the day He died

When His disciples all forsook Him
He walked alone
On the road that day
As He carried your cross
Down the via's way
He was alone
The day the angels cried

Rebekah Hayler:
He was God's Son, the One who came
To save the souls
Of those that would kill Him
Lamb of God sent to be slain
For all your sins
He longs to forgive them
He is the Father's only Son
Yet He and His Father's will are one
And He was alone
The day the angels cried

lst Chorus - Duet
Freddy Hayler:
On the cross He cried, "My Father

Rebekah Hayler:
Abba, Father, do not forsake Me."

Freddy Hayler:
Left alone to die for you and for me
His blood flowed down that tree for our sins

Rebekah Hayler:
Alone on the cross
As they cut Him down
The devil's laughter filled
The dark sky
Thunder and lightning
Struck the ground
As the earth quaked forth
From the final battle

Freddy Hayler:
As He became sin on the cross that day
The Father's face
Just turned away
And He was alone
The day the angels cried

2nd Chorus - Duet
Rebekah Hayler:
Then they laid Him in a dark tomb
For three days was left alone there

Freddy Hayler:
But on the third day
God, the Father, cried,
"Jesus, My Son,
Come and rise
In Your victory over death and hell."
In Jesus alone the victory's won
For He was alone
The day the angels
The angels rejoice

Rebekah Hayler:
Now lift up your voice
Freddy Hayler:
For as Christ the Lord ascended
Rebekah Hayler:
Our redemption now is granted

Freddy Hayler:
And the angels understand
God's great salvation plan
Can you hear them rejoice?

[Piano Interlude]

Freddy Hayler:
Now I can say
By the grace of God
He's in my heart
To dwell forever
Jesus, the music of my life
Forget all your past and dead
**   tradition**
Jesus alone is the living way
All the angels rejoice when
Just one is saved
So be free from your sin
Receive Him
Receive Him
Receive Christ today
Rebekah Hayler:
Jesus is the Way!

Rebekah and Freddy Hayler:
Jesus is the Way!
Make Him Lord today!
Rebekah Hayler:
Jesus is the Way!

This Is Your Day

G. Felisatti - Malise - Malise G. Nuti
English Lyrics: Freddy Hayler

I dedicate this song to all of you who need a miracle touch from God this very day!

"The yoke shall be destroyed because of the anointing" (Isaiah 10:27).

"Then a cloud covered the tent of the congregation, and the glory of the Lord filled the tabernacle" (Exodus 40:34).

He's here,
I can feel His presence now
For His Spirit without measure
Now flows from heaven above
For in Jesus we have come to
Praise and honor Him

He said
That where two or three agree
Who have gathered in His name
His sweet anointing would come
We have come into His presence

To praise and worship Him

1st Chorus
And declare His majesty
Our Prince and Lord Supreme
He has brought down the gates of
  hell
And risen from the dead
Declare His majesty
And lift your voices to the King
This is your day to touch the glory
His glory!

Yes, here
I can see His glory now
And He sees you who are burdened
Why don't you touch His glory now
Jesus sees your need and He
  loves you
By faith, receive from Him

2nd Chorus
And declare His Majesty
There's healing in His wings

53

This is your day for miracles!
Your faith has made you
  whole!
Declare His majesty!
And lift your hands unto the King
This is your day to touch the glory!

Interlude
This is your day to touch the glory
Of His majesty!

Eternal God [Song of Metatron]

Music: Paul Sjolund - Freddy Hayler
Lyrics: Freddy Hayler

"The eternal God is thy refuge, and underneath are the everlasting arms: and he shall thrust out the enemy from before thee" (Deuteronomy 33:27).

"For thus saith the high and lofty One that inhabiteth eternity, whose name is Holy; I dwell in the high and holy place, with him also that is of a contrite and humble spirit, to revive the spirit of the humble, and to revive the heart of the contrite ones" (Isaiah 57:15).

"Now unto the King eternal, immortal, invisible, the only wise God, be honour and glory for ever and ever. Amen" (1 Timothy 1:17).

1st Chorus
Eternal God
Of love who has no ending
Humbly I bow
To worship at Your throne
That we may see
Your glory all transcendent
Create in me
A temple for Your throne

Verse 1
Glory and honor unto Your name
I lift my hands to Thee
To give You praise
Now let Your river flow
A mighty stream
Of healing waters
Cleanse, heal, relieve

2nd Chorus
Eternal God
Of love who knows no ending
Humbly we bow
To worship at Your throne
That we may see
Your glory all transcendent
Create in me
A temple for Your own

Eternal God
Eternal Life
Eternal Love

From "Eternal Love"
Arrangement: Freddy Hayler
Publishing: 2001 Walton Music Corporation, ASCAP
Lyrics: ©Crystal Sea Publishing 2001
2001 Song of Angels® Project, Vol. 1

"I AM THAT I AM" (EXODUS 3:14).

Message [The Burning Bush]

Glory!
Glory to the eternally self-
  existent One!
All-consuming holy fire
Who purifies our souls
You who spoke to Moses
  through
The burning bush
You who delivered the Israelites
Through the Red Sea
Into the Promised Land
You who raised Jesus Christ
From the dead
You who give us eternal life
God of love
God of hope
Eternal God

From "Eternal Love"
Arrangement: Freddy Hayler
Publishing: 1984 Walton Music
Corporation, ASCAP
Lyrics: ©Crystal Sea Publishing 2001

A Celestial Odyssey

From "The Vision"
Malise
English Lyrics: Freddy Hayler

Late one evening while deep in worship, in a vision of the night, I saw in the Spirit an enormous angel ten times larger than the most physical and muscular man I had ever seen on this earth. He had golden, curly hair, with eyes like liquid blue lightning. His face was like that of a shining, white-hot furnace, and in his mouth were tongues of fire from which came forth beautiful, celestial languages of the heavens. Suddenly, his right hand extended upward toward the northern sky, while his left hand clasped the end of a brilliant, bright, glowing amber sword.

His clothes were made of a heavenly material—such as not ever found or seen on this earth— like a very fine, bead-like material that seemed as if it were alive. Platinum-like in color, it pulsated with light, a living light that emanated the very glory of my Creator God.

Oh, and sundry and ever-changing musical melodies in endless scales and descants of indescribable beauty were like a spontaneous spring gushing forth from his very garments.

I began to realize that this angelic being had just come from the presence of almighty God, for the glory beads of His garment still sparkled and shimmered with the light of God's own Shekinah presence. I trembled at the reality and the very existence of such glorious beings obviously from another

©2001 Thomas Blackshear II

NO. 13

dimension far greater than this. His face was imbued with a spirit of nobility and purity and purpose, and yet with an almost pitiful expression, he looked down on my trembling frame and said with a loud, clarion voice, "Come."

He took me by the hand, and in one moment we were moving upward at great speed. I could see a great throne of light on the horizon to the north. All around the throne was a brilliant fog and mist, surrounded by incalculably tall, towering clouds with a multitude of lightnings and loud thunders. I could see angelic beings singing beautiful songs, and some were doing cartwheels in the sky.

Again on the horizon one could easily see in the far distance a glorious throne, upon which sat the most excellent, glorious God and King. Above His throne was an emerald rainbow, the arc of which is immeasurable in height, too awesome to describe. To the northeast, I could clearly see seven large, jeweled mountains with pillars of holy fire extending up from them.

The angel said, "This is the future dwelling place prepared for God's own elect." I then pleaded with the angel, "Please take me closer to God's throne," because I could feel the life, the love, and the light that came from His very being, even though it was at such a far-off distance. The closer we drew, the more alive I felt—the more joy I experienced. I never felt so alive in my entire existence. God is the source of all life, love, holiness, and perfection. To be close to Him is an unutterable ecstasy.

And as we drew closer, I trembled with fear, for I began to see the four beasts. These powerful, cherubim-like, living creatures, protect the throne of God and incessantly praise the Lord of the universe. I could see the multitude of their eyes, within and without, that see and discern all things. One is not capable of perceiving or calculating their height, their width, their fearsome might or power, or the amplitude of their energy or strength.

Glory and honor! A great throng of angelic symphonies continuously play free-flowing music. As I looked upward, I could see streaking across the celestial skies of heaven, like shooting stars, multitudes of chariots of multiple colors carrying scores of heavenly luminaries. And I could see a sea of angelic beings—seraphim, cherubim, archangels, and angels of all varieties—a multitude too numerous to estimate, all raising their hands and playing instruments to the glory of Him who sits on the throne amid the four beasts.

Myriads of angels sang with such beautiful and glorious singing; millions of angelic voices blended together in descants so high and harmonious and complex, with such amazing ethereal quality as to defy the imagination.

Suddenly, there appeared to the right side of the throne One who had the appearance as unto the Son of Man. In an instant, the angel and I fell prostrate on the crystal floor as if slain, while a great archangel exclaimed with a loud voice, "Behold, the Son of

God. Worship Him!" The brilliance of the Shekinah streamed forth from His presence for millions and millions of earth miles.

And with voice of many waters, the archangel said, "Let him who has ears hear what Jesus Christ has to say to His church."

Jesus said, "Happy is he who turns aside from the pride of this life, the lusts of the flesh—and who forsakes the secular, ungodly paths of this fallen cosmos, and lucifer, the fallen one!"

Then, suddenly, I heard peals of the loudest thunders and huge lightnings. Heavenly whirlwinds pushed us higher and higher toward the Most Holy One's very own throne. No flesh can directly behold the Father's face or see His form. No evil will dwell in His presence. No man, no flesh, can or will glory in His presence. Yet the extent of the holy Father is incomprehensible and without measure or analogy.

To see this part of the vision was for me to melt into nothingness. I cried out to the angel, "Please, save my life!" For the lips of the Lord are as a furnace of fire. There is no metaphor or words in earthly language to describe all this. The face of our God cannot be spoken of. Yet from His glorious face, He emits sparks and lightnings of life for the entire universe. The light of the face of God is brighter than a trillion sun-stars. His holy face is like a man's, but it is translucent and incandescent, and so unutterably beautiful and pleasurable beyond any comparison. His face is supremely awesome and infinitely unique and glorious, with powerful and mighty mysterious voices of incomprehensible magnitudes, multiple voices and billions of commands, simultaneous commands, coming forth from His mouth and being. His form is attended to by armies of millions of angels who obey His every pulse of thought and whim, who do His bidding and worship His holy face with unending singing. The glory of the omnipotent, eternal One is dazzling beyond description.

Then this marvelous archangel looked down upon me and said, "Yet even the least of the elect saints are the brothers and sisters of Jesus Christ, your Lord. Yea, even you shall sing a song that we angelic beings can never sing. For by the blood of Jesus Christ, you have been adopted and made part of the royal family of God, and you will sing forever the song of the redeemed, and shall rule and reign with our God!"

I still remember the vision and can almost recall the glorious sounds of His angels. For with the angels' song I again can see His throne. Glory! Glory to Him forever and ever! Glory to Jesus! May I sing to You and praise You with the angels! The angels worship You and adore You!

Glory to the Lamb!

Vision of Freddy Hayler, Christmas Eve From "Rapsodia"
©2001 Insieme S.r.l./Zucchero & Fornaciari Music S.r.l.
Published in U.S.A. by Sugar-Melodi, Inc. 2001 Song of Angels® Project, Vol. 1

NO. 15

Epiphany…the Return

F. Sartori - L. Quarantotto
English Lyrics: Freddy Hayler

I see You now
Shekinah all around You
Adoring angels praise You
Before Your throne
I see glory
Glory in the highest
And an emerald rainbow
Round the throne of God
And a crystal river
Now flowing from Your presence
With Your love and healing
For all the nations

And He'll cause your mind to see
And open the deaf ears
To hear the angels singing to
 Him
And you know you're His
And He's yours
And we will shout for joy
For we have seen His glory!
And immediately after the vision
And upon returning to the
earthly realm
I pray our eyes are open
To see the extreme need for
 holiness
Heaven is a place of purity,
 glory, and light
Oh, how He loves you
And He wants you to be with Him
For all eternity
He'll never stop loving you
You are His bride
Prepare yourself for Him!

Choir

Eyes a liquid flame of fire
The holy Lamb shines brighter
Than a billion angels above
Lift your hands and praise your
 King
And we will shout for joy
For we have seen His glory!

CRYSTAL CHRISTIANITY

Enthroned above myriads of faces,
crowned in golden diadem
bright as jasper and clear as quartz,
eyes blazing like coals
through an emerald rainbow,
the King gazes down
to transparent forms
burning from within;
shining in a sea of glass,
they mirror His glory:
every gentle word
or graceful wave of His hand
caresses their will—
love obeys where Love reigns;
the crucial flame
in a purifying crucible
is obedience.
Crystal Christians brighten earth;
though darkness crowds round,
the Light shines—
it cannot be overcome!

—David L. Young

Crystal Christianity

About the front cover art: *A Vision in the Night*

"There, in the night sky, beyond the starlight, in a vision…."

he front cover art is not to be construed as an actual representation of God's throne, but is a similitude of a vision given to me while praying and meditating on the passage of Revelation 4:3. The illustration is symbolic of a vision the Lord gave me late one evening on Christmas Eve. The dark, starry sky represents the actual stars I was gazing upon that evening. As God's light began to permeate the night firmament, I became intensely aware of the brightness, majesty, and glory of God's throne. His glorious light pierced the darkness of that night sky in a way that I will never forget! Yes, God is light (John 1:4–8)!

A Divine Litmus Test

"When a prophet speaketh in the name of the LORD, if the thing follow not, nor comes to pass, that is the thing which the LORD hath not spoken" (Deuteronomy 18:22).

In Joel 2:22 and Acts 2:16–18, the Bible speaks of the Holy Spirit in the last days giving visions and dreams to confirm God's Word and to cause us to seek His face. True Christians should be concerned with deceptions, counterfeits, and spiritual misguidance. (See Exodus 7:11–13; 22:18; Leviticus 19:31; 20:27; Deuteronomy 18:9–12; Jeremiah 27:9–10.) All dreams and visions must be tested to see if they confirm Holy Scripture, pass the test of spiritually mature leadership, and point people to Jesus and to Jesus alone.

"Let the prophets speak two or three, and let the others judge" (1 Corinthians 14:29).

Yet God has promised to speak to His

people even in this day through men and women of God who are in tune with the Scriptures and the Holy Spirit. Jesus is the same yesterday, today, and forever (Hebrews 13:8)! God spoke to Moses in the book of Exodus, and to Agabus in the book of Acts (Acts 11:28; 21:10); in the same manner, He still speaks today in order to confirm His Word or some new prophetic event.

"Hear now my words: If there be a prophet among you, I the LORD will make myself known unto him in a vision, and will speak unto him in a dream" (Numbers 12:6).

The outpouring of the supernatural presence of God, the general understanding of the universe, and increased angelic activity are definitely biblical signs of the last days. Some "intellectual" Christians, who are cessationist/dispensationalists, deny the supernatural gifts of God for today (1 Corinthians 12–14). The other extreme is just as unbalanced. This is when people base their life decisions solely on "direct" supernatural revelations. But God desires both biblical and experiential revelation to guide us in all His truth. All experiential revelation that is God-inspired will always confirm and never contradict inerrant Scripture.

There are specific, detailed things about heaven, other dimensions of reality, science, and other facts about God and His creation that the Bible is silent on. This does not mean that He cannot directly reveal some of these aspects of His reality to earnest believers. He desires us to worship Him in spirit and truth (John 4:23–24). God wants your whole heart. He wants to fellowship with you in the holiest place. He wants you to become a worshipper so that He can impart His glory and abundance into your life and show you many new things about Himself!

The Vision and the Artwork

"And he that sat was to look upon like a jasper and sardine stone: and there was a rainbow around the throne, in sight like unto an emerald" (Revelation 4:3).

In Revelation 21:19–21 and Exodus 28:15 and 17:20, there are cryptic language and meanings behind the Scriptures that make an undeniable claim that all glory, praise, and honor are due to Jesus and Jesus alone! It is apparent that each of the jewels that fashion the foundation of the Celestial City correspond to the names of the twelve tribes of Israel. We see in Genesis 35:18 and 24, and 29:32–35 that the Hebrew meaning of the names of the twelve tribes of Israel not only corresponded to the jewels on the high priest's ephod, but also corre-

spond to the gemstone foundation of the new heavenly Jerusalem (Revelation 21:19–20)! The meaning that God gives these names is not without significance and has much to do with the vision I have had regarding the meaning of Revelation 4:3.

Heavenly Symbolism

In the Bible, jasper stone is representative of Benjamin, the sardius stone is representative of the tribe of Reuben, and the emerald is symbolic of the tribe of Judah. (See Genesis 35:18–24; 29:32–35.) In other words, the glorious message of the front cover illustration is this:

Benjamin (jasper): "Here is the Son of My right hand"

Reuben (sardius): "Behold, a vision of the Son! The firstborn and only begotten royal One of kingly and priestly origin"

Judah (emerald): "Behold, the saving strength of My right hand, the Lion who has conquered, the preeminent One full of majesty and glory. All His brethren shall praise Him!"

In other words, no man or woman will glory in His presence. No flesh will glory in His presence. No evil will dwell in His presence (Psalm 5:4–5). In the book of Revelation, the apostle John saw the people of God over and over as worshippers (Revelation 5:11–13). A lot of good Christian people study the book of Revelation primarily as an esoteric, apocalyptic, eschatalogical Bible book of end-times prophecies, when in fact the central message throughout Revelation is profoundly simple: Worship the Lord Jesus Christ only, for He alone is worthy. The entire book of Revelation is the revelation of Jesus Christ and a declaration to worship Him! Even the jeweled construction materials of heaven are transparent or translucent, so that all things there will reflect and emanate the light rays and beams of God's glory. Therefore, let us become worshippers so that our new heavenly home in the Celestial City of God will already be a familiar place to us as believers when we arrive!

Repentance Needed

But we must first lay aside our sinful cloaks of self-deception and allow our hearts to be exposed to His holy radiation. Let us with humility and honesty allow the Word of God to cleanse our hearts from lies. May we allow the Holy Spirit to break the power of pride and self-deception in our lives. Jesus said in Luke 8:15 that all good fruit-bearers of His kingdom will have honest and pure hearts. Therefore, as we celebrate the church's mission in the twenty-first century, let us also repent so that we may experience the greatest harvest the church has ever known in

over two thousand years! Let us now go forth in the radiant light rays of God's glory!

The Invisible War

The end-times reformation people of God will understand that their strongest battle is a spiritual one. Brother, you do not have a financial problem; you have a spiritual one! Sister, you do not have a marital problem; you have a spiritual problem! We must learn to war against the principalities and powers of darkness that have set themselves to destroy us. Elisha's servant needed his eyes to be opened to see that the true spiritual battle was God's to win (2 Kings 6:17). Yet many of us are more like Saul of Tarsus, whose carnal eyes are blinded. We need our eyes to be opened (Acts 9:8, 18).

Ephesians 6:12 tells us that *"we wrestle not against flesh and blood, but against principalities, against powers, against the rulers of the darkness of this world, against spiritual wickedness in high places."* In Revelation 12:7, we see the angels who are daily fighting the real battle in the heavenlies on behalf of the church of the Lord Jesus Christ. We also see Michael, the other great archangels, and the innumerable army of angels who fight the devil and his dark minions in response to the intercessions and prayers of the true saints. (See Daniel 10: 2–16.)

Personal Encounters

It wasn't until my lovely wife, Annie, encountered a ten-foot-tall angel in our home that I first got a revelation of the reality of these magnificent celestial beings. Several years ago, after an extended fast and intercession for the salvation of a lost neighbor of ours, she literally (not figuratively) described them to me in vivid detail. Little did I know that one recent

Christmas Eve, while my own life was in deep struggle and frustration, I would have a trancelike vision of heavenly angels from which the lyrics of this album were birthed. Why did these visions occur?

The True Prophetic
Gives You a Biblical Destiny

God wants us to know that we are destined for His throne. He wants us to know that the time is short. He wants you to feel a divine sense of urgency. He wants you to do something uniquely great for Him so that you may have eternal reward and will not be ashamed at His coming. He is preparing for Himself a bride that is pure and without spot (Ephesians 5:27). (The Greek word used here for *spot* is *spilos,* referring to a spot or stain, and is used metaphorically to represent a moral blemish, as in a lascivious and riotous person.) We are admonished to hate the garment that is spotted by the fallen, carnal nature and to be free from all defilement in the sight of God. *"God is no respecter of persons"* (Acts 10:34). It doesn't matter if you are Anglican, Catholic, Orthodox, Evangelical, Pentecostal, Charismatic Full Gospel, Lutheran, Episcopalian, Methodist, Presbyterian, Baptist, AME, Assemblies of God, Messianic Jew, or Independent. You are to keep the commandments of Jesus without alteration in their fulfillment. (See 1 Timothy 6:14; James 1:27; 2 Peter 3:14.) Jesus said, *"If ye love me, keep my commandments"* (John 14:15). The commandments of Christ are not grievous (1 John 5:3). The law of God is the law of love (Matthew 22:37).

It matters not what any man preaches or what any person says. Many people today have religious opinions and will say to you, "Oh, such-and-such is a good thing," or "So-and-so is a good person." But only God can define what is good, and He has done so through His law and through unbending, axiomatic Bible revelation! Let us not be deceived. God's goal is *"that he might present it to himself a glorious church, not having spot, or wrinkle, or any such thing; but that it should be holy and without blemish"* (Ephesians 5:27).

Speaking of His bride, the church, Jesus says, *"Thou art all fair, my love; there is no spot in thee"* (Song of Solomon 4:7). He is preparing for Himself a bride without spot and wrinkle. He's not preparing spots for Himself! God's plans for your destiny are for good.

"For I know the thoughts that I think toward you, saith the LORD, thoughts of peace, and not of evil, to give you an expected end" (Jeremiah 29:11).

God Hates "Mixture"

We need to separate ourselves from evil and worldly influences. This does not mean that we are to become reclusive in an ascetic sense. It also doesn't mean that we don't reach out to the worst of sinners. However, it does mean that we do not copy or emulate in our lifestyle the ungodly, pagan influences of popular culture. In fact, popular culture operates under entirely different moral principles than the kingdom of God. To become "relevant" does not necessarily mean to become like the culture we are trying to reach, if those aspects of culture are sinful.

> **"The Holy Ghost cannot conquer the world with unbelief, nor can He save the world with a worldly church. For this enterprise, He wants a separated, sanctified, sacrificial people."**
> **—Samuel Chadwick**

Bloch

Plate B

> **"If revival is being withheld from us, it is because some worldly idol remains still enthroned; because we still insist on placing our reliance in human schemes; because we still refuse to face the unchangeable truth that it is not by might, but by God's Spirit."**
> **—Jonathan Goforth**

"The word of the LORD came unto me, saying, Son of man, the house of Israel is to me become dross: all they are brass, and tin, and iron, and lead, in the midst of the furnace; they are even the dross of silver. Therefore thus saith the Lord GOD; Because ye are all become dross, behold, therefore I will gather you into the midst of Jerusalem. As they gather silver, and brass, and iron, and lead, and tin, into the midst of the furnace, to blow the fire upon it, to melt it; so will I gather you in mine anger and in my fury, and I will leave you there, and melt you. Yea, I will, gather you, and blow upon you in the fire of my wrath....Son of man, say unto her, Thou art the land that is not cleansed" (Ezekiel 22:17–21, 24).

"Lip service" and "easy believism" will not be enough to make it spiritually in these days. Many say "I love God," but if they continue in habitual sins (as opposed to occasional sins repented of) and they have consistent, unrepentant disobedience in any area of their lives, they have reason to be concerned about their spiritual destiny. Yes, Jesus is a lover of your soul, but habitual sin is a killer to your soul. Satan and sin are serial killers! We are to hate sin with a passion. The devil has come to kill, steal, and destroy, but Jesus has come that we might have life and life more abundantly (John 10:10). True Christianity is to love God, to love our neighbor, and to love His liberating moral laws with all our hearts (Matthew 22:37–39; Psalm 119). This heart attitude will prepare us to dwell with Him in fellowship for all eternity. Like Jesus our Lord, we need to love righteousness and hate iniquity (Hebrews 1:9). Jesus said, *"Blessed are the pure in heart: for they shall see God"* (Matthew 5: 8).

> **"All practical power over sin and over men depends on maintaining closet communion. Those who abide in the secret place with God show themselves mighty to conquer evil....They are seers who read His secrets and know His will."**
> **—A. T. Pierson**

The Power of Innocence

"Then said Daniel unto the king....My God hath sent his angel, and hath shut the lions' mouths, that they have not hurt me: forasmuch as before him **innocency** *was found in me; and also before thee, O king, I have done no hurt"* (Daniel 6:21–22, emphasis added).

Too many professing Christians today are too knowledgeable and refined in their understanding of evil, the ways of satan, and the world system he controls. Paul said that we're to be innocent or ignorant of evil, but wise concerning righteousness (Romans 16:19). Too many professing Christians have already become jaded and hardened by their worldly knowledge of sin. They have imbibed too much filth, violence, and occultism. Their souls, like sponges, have absorbed inordinate amounts of evil—demonic imaginations created by Hollywood, television and movie writers, and producers. Some have already become addicted to filthy, pornographic Internet sites. They are not anonymous. God sees all!

Unsanctified man's propensity to look upon evil has opened the door for an innumerable army of unclean devils and evil spirits to take residence in people's minds as strongholds of bondage and lust. Their eyes cannot

cease from sin. They have defiled themselves with the spirit of baal. Because of this, many Christian leaders in recent years have been falling away from the faith on a large scale. If you have stumbled in your walk with God, I beseech you, let God restore you to childlike innocence and purity. No heart is too hard that He cannot cleanse it through the blood of Jesus! He loves you! He will cast your evil imaginations and sins into the deepest part of the sea, never to be remembered anymore (Psalm 51:1–10; 103:12). Now that's grace! (See 1 John 1:7, 9.)

Power in Purity

Daniel's secret to personal purity was both in private intercession and in keeping himself pure from the Babylonian lifestyles and practices of his day. It didn't mean he became a recluse or retreated to a monastery. Rather, his secret was in his passion for the presence of God in his life, and that hunger in Daniel determined his great future (Daniel 1:8–9; 6:10; 10:12). God supernaturally intervened to stop the mouths of lions on behalf of the young prophet Daniel because innocence and purity of heart were found in him (Daniel 6:21–22). Did not Jesus say the same in Matthew 10:16? The reason most Christians today experience little supernatural power in their lives is that sin blocks the free flow of God's Holy Spirit.

Christian Radiation

He wants to make us pure, holy, transparent vessels that have the capacity to handle His great power and love, so that a lost world can see His glory and light brilliantly reflecting in us—all of us like sanctified, flawless, jeweled prisms reflecting all the colors of His love, holiness, character, and divine at-tributes. We don't have to wait until the redemption of our bodies and the Wedding Supper of the Lamb to experience fulfilling our destinies in Christ. It is my prayer that, as you listen to *Song of Angels®* and read this little book, God will lovingly whisper to you, His beloved, how much He loves your uniqueness and your differences. As a consecrated vessel, you were created to have divine purpose in His agenda for reaching the earth today. It doesn't matter how much education you have, how much money you have, whether you've been the victim of divorce or some other tragedy, what your racial background is, what nation you are from—all that matters is that you have a heart to become a pure, yielded vessel to the Bridegroom. Then and only then will the powerful, life-changing light rays and beams of God's *kabod* radiate and shoot forth from your life to bring healing, deliverance, and salvation to those who dwell in physical and spiritual darkness around you.

"Arise, shine; for thy light is come, and the glory of the LORD is risen upon thee. For, behold, the darkness shall cover the earth, and gross darkness the people: but the LORD shall arise upon thee, and his glory shall be seen upon thee. And the Gentiles shall come to thy light, and kings to the brightness of thy rising. Lift up thine eyes round about, and see: all they gather themselves together, they come to thee: thy sons shall come from far, and thy daughters shall be nursed at thy side" (Isaiah 60:1–4).

Casting "Shadows"

God desires the "shadow" of His presence to operate in and through us on a daily basis. In Acts 5:14–16, the shadow of Peter was in fact God's glorious radiation, His very presence emanating from Peter's body, bringing deliverance to those possessed by devils, bound by sickness and disease, and shackled by mental oppression and

"The Transfiguration" Plate C

habitual sins. Is this not the true ministry of Jesus—to set the captives free and bring liberty to those in bondage (Isaiah 61:1–3; Acts 10:38)? Is this not what end-times reformation Christianity should be? A veritable spiritual nuclear explosion of God's glory is coming upon the church in order to empower believers. This explosion will inevitably radiate the knowledge of His glory to all the nations (Habakkuk 2:14)!

Transparency

God desires moral clearness of spirit, soul, and body (1 Thessalonians 5:23). We should fervently desire those in spiritual darkness to come to know, through us, the salvation that is in Jesus Christ alone (Acts 4:12). We should call them to join with the angels singing on the crystal sea—a sea glittery, dazzling, glistening with the reflections of God's Shekinah presence—where the life, power, and glory of God flow through a crystal river that quenches the thirst of those who seek eternal life and glory. Therefore, there is a great need in each of us as God's saints for clearness, purity, and transparency of heart and life, where no sin can cloud or block the light rays and beams of God's glory shooting forth from us to shine upon a world darkened by sin. The Bible says that we are to emanate God's light; for *"God is light"* (1 John 1:5), and if we are transparent, people will see God in us. God is preparing us in clarity and truth. A famous Christian astrophysicist has said, "He is preparing us for life in the full light of His glory (sunglasses no longer needed)."

> "By the time the average Christian gets his temperature up to normal, everybody thinks he has a fever!"
>
> —Watchman Nee

NO. 22

Fire on You!

The Bible says that God is *"a consuming fire"* (Hebrews 12:29). Our glorified Jesus now has eyes of liquid fire (Revelation 1:12–16)! Therefore, those of you who live continually in His presence will become like Him—fiery and transparent!

> **"We need the dynamic of a flaming ministry that will set the church on fire."**
> **—Samuel M. Zwemer**

I ask you, therefore, are you combustible? Are you saturated with the oil of the Holy Spirit of God? Are you ignitable? The devout missionary, Amy Carmichael, once prayed, "Make me thy fuel, O flame of God!"

Consider John Wesley's view of holiness: "I set myself on fire, and the people come to see me burn."

And again, through the Holy Spirit the prophet Isaiah said, *"Arise, shine; for thy light is come, and the glory of the LORD is risen upon thee. For, behold, the darkness shall cover the earth, and gross darkness the people: but the LORD shall arise upon thee, and his glory shall be seen upon thee. And the Gentiles shall come to thy light, and kings to the brightness of thy rising"* (Isaiah 60:1–3).

The apostle John said, *"God is light"* (1 John 1:5).

"In him was life; and the life was the light of men. And the light shineth in darkness; and the darkness comprehended it not. There was a man sent from God, whose name was John. The same came for a witness, to bear witness of the Light, that all men through him might believe. He was not that Light, but was sent to bear witness of that Light. That was the true Light, which lighteth every man that cometh into the world. (John 1:4–9).

Then spake Jesus again unto them, say-

ing, *I am the light of the world: he that followeth me shall not walk in darkness, but shall have the light of life*" (John 8:12).

Shine, Jesus, Shine

Therefore, if we as believers are clear and transparent, what will the world see in us? They will see God! Clearness! Transparency! The keys to world missions! We have worldwide radio and satellite TV ministries, a plethora of ministry conventions and seminars, huge evangelistic crusades and Bible training centers. We have high-tech Internet churches, missiological methods, cross-cultural strategies, linguistics, and church growth methodologies, and all of this is wonderful. But how much more powerful would all of it be if it would be enjoined with holiness, personal transparency, and supernatural power?

Paul said, "*And my speech and my preaching were not with persuasive words of human wisdom, but in demonstration of the Spirit and of power, that your faith should not be in the wisdom* [or technology!] *of men but in the power of God*" (1 Corinthians 2:4–5 NKJV).

Are we not living epistles read by all men (2 Corinthians 3:2)? I attended two of the most prestigious evangelical seminaries in the land, and I can tell you firsthand that book knowledge; clever homiletics; having a winsome, charismatic personality, keen wit, and so on, does not and cannot meet the spiritual needs and hunger of God's people in this hour. Only the supernatural presence of a holy God can deliver! Only by the anointing is the yoke broken (Isaiah 10:27)!

"Retro" Ministry

Jesus' methods are simple but profound—profound simplicity! When Jesus ministered on earth, neither He nor the disciples had any mass media or slick advertising groups promoting Him. They were not highly polished wordsmiths or modernistic editors. No one ghostwrote for Jesus and His disciples. They did not use catchy phrases replete with fine graphics and attention-getting blurbs. There were no TV or radio ministry broadcasts. There was no mass printing and mailing available. Yet Jesus and this small group of disciples changed the world forever through their transparent, holy lives and ministries. *"God is no respecter of persons"* (Acts 10:34). Jesus wants His supernatural works to shine through you! Jesus said, *"Greater works than these shall* [you] *do"* (John 14:12). God desires you to become a sign and a wonder to the world (Isaiah 8:18). This is not a metaphor or symbolic language. God means what He says!

World Missions: God's Priority

Again, it bears repeating that the time is urgent (Matthew 24:14). All of us are called to participate, in one form or another, in world missions (Matthew 28:18–20). The more on fire we become for Jesus and the more we evangelize in a spirit of holiness, the more we will hasten the day of His return by reaching all the nations for Christ. God had only one Son, and He was a missionary (John 3:16–17)! We should have such hearts burdened for souls!

The Call

Many people today ask, "How can I know my call? What is my ministry?" As an inner-city-New-York Sunday school evangelist has stated, "If you want to know your ministry, then your ministry is when God shows you a need, then you go and meet that need." Someone may need a job, someone may need to be healed, someone may need to be encouraged in prison, someone may need groceries, someone may need clothes or medicine, someone may need a tract with the the Good News, someone may need you to listen to their problems and to pray for them. Some of you may be called to a specific nation to preach the Gospel or to plant a church or to do medical missions. But each of you is called to participate in winning souls to Christ and at least in some capacity to support or pray for missionaries to all the nations. Each of us is uniquely designed by God for a specific purpose. God has created each one differently, and He ardently loves those differences. The specific talents He has given you as an individual are the point of your strength.

Every joint does supply (Ephesians 4:16)! All of us have been given giftings and callings from the Lord. Each of you has a particular deposit God has invested in you for the healing of the nations. Take heed not to bury His gifts in the sands of selfishness and the fear of man (Proverbs 29:25; Matthew 25:24–30).

God's Heart Is for Missions

Ninety percent of the world's preachers preach to five percent of the world's population! This is not right before God. No one has an excuse for this. God has blessed us with too many blessings. *Everyone* can lay hands on the sick! *Everyone* can tell someone the good news of the Gospel. Everyone can encourage someone who is discouraged. So why have over three billion souls never heard the Gospel? Why are there more people in the Amway and Avon sales forces than all the active missionaries in the evangelical and Catholic churches combined? Are we afraid to admit the truth? In fact, because of the fear of man, many do not want to serve God in the highest call, nor do they want to win souls. *"The fear of man bringeth a snare; but whoso putteth his trust in the* LORD *shall be safe"* (Proverbs 29:25).

> **"The greatest hindrances to the evangelization of the world are those within the church."**
> **—John R. Mott**

Selfish fear is based on pride and a spirit of self-preservation. But Jesus said, "He who seeks to save his life will lose it." (See Matthew 16:25.) As Oswald Smith has said, "No one has the right to hear the Gospel twice while there remains someone who has never heard it once." Consider what Charles H. Spurgeon said: "There are two types of Christians—soulwinners and backsliders." O backslider, God is married to you and longs for His prodigals to return to Him.

Let us have the heart of father Abraham, who was willing to leave his familiar culture and family ties and go to a nation he had never heard of, all because God gave him a vision and showed him a need. Genesis 12:1–6 is, in fact, the first Great Commission in the Word of God. Abraham saw the heavenly Father's desire for a chosen nation. Brothers and sisters in Christ, when Jesus shows you a need, you need to obey! But how can you obey if you do not *hear* your call (Romans 1:1, 6), *know* your call, *prepare* for your call (2 Timothy 1:9; 4:5), *enter* your call, and then *abide* in your call (2 Corinthians 7:22–24)? Only after you have taken these steps can you *"make full proof of thy ministry"* (2 Timothy 4:5). This process of obedience all starts with being sensitive to the burden of the Holy Spirit to love your neighbor. When God shows you his or her need, answer the call. Your neighbor may be next door, or he may be in Mongolia. God commands you to love your neighbor as yourself (Matthew 19:19; 22:39).

Love's Constraining Power

"For the love of Christ constraineth us" (2 Corinthians 5:14).

George Whitfield and John Wesley, by preaching a sermon called "The Almost Christian," convincingly proved how we, without operating under the law of love toward God and our neighbor, are in fact *almost* Christians and not *altogether* Christians. These two preachers also taught that six of the Ten Com-mandments are manward and neighborward, while four are Godward. They emphatically proved that God placed a strong emphasis on loving and reaching out to those those around you with a missionary heart. Indeed, God had only one Son, and He was a missionary!

"Go for souls, and go for the worst."
—William Booth

"For God so loved the world, that he gave his only begotten Son, that whosoever believeth in him should not perish, but have everlasting life. For God sent not his Son into the world to condemn the world; but that the world through him might be saved" (John 3:16–17)

How many of us are willing to give ourselves to missions work, to inner-city and urban ministry, to a soup kitchen or the back dusty roads of Central Amer-ica? All of us cannot actually go and do missions work at once, but we can all participate in prayer and in strategic support of such mandated outreach. Many of us can no longer serve God in "safe" havens of suburban American homes isolated from human need. There are thousands of unreached people groups in this world that await the revelation of Jesus Christ through you!

"For all have sinned, and come short of the glory of God" (Romans 3:23).

"The wages of sin is death; but the gift of God is eternal life through Jesus Christ

our Lord" (Romans 6:23).

"*But as many as received him, to them gave he power to become the sons of God*" (John 1:12).

"*Behold, I stand at the door, and knock: if any man hear my voice, and open the door, I will come in to him*" (Revelation 3:20).

The "Glory Look"

Iridescent, transparent reformation people will act like the first-century disciples of Christ, even though they live in the twenty-first century. Brother and sister, you need bioluminescence in your life! When Moses came down from the mount after an intimate encounter with God, he experienced the bioluminescence of God's Shekinah glory!

It bears repeating again and again that Jesus is preparing a bride without spot or wrinkle—flawless. He is purging us with the holy fires of heaven, setting us aglow with His Shekinah presence. For the countenance of such glory will shine upon your face even as it did upon the faces of Moses and Stephen (Exodus 34:29; Acts 6:15). Then both Jew and Gentile will see God's glory living in us as holy temples, and they will come to the knowledge of His salvation (1 Peter 2:9–12)!

Our cry should be, "Lord Jesus, purge us by Your fire. Cleanse us by Your blood. Baptize us in the Holy Spirit, and fill us with a love and zeal in order that we may inherit that crystal Celestial City, the New Jerusalem. There, no sin can dwell; there, all the inhabitants and all the things existing within are clear and transparent in order to reflect the light rays and beams of God's glory; there, all souls engraved on God's hand will live in sinless perfection and love. Amen!

The Bridegroom Is Coming!

On two separate occasions I have seen a huge supernova-like explosion breaking forth from the middle star of the constellation Orion. (See Job 9:9; 38:31; Amos 5:8.) I saw this in both an open vision and in a dream. I then asked the Lord, "Why Orion?" What significance did this have?

The awesome constellations of the Milky Way arrayed before our eyes by our Creator God tell of the eternal story of redemption. The night sky is one of the best Bible tracts God ever created! (See Psalm 8:3–5; Romans 1:20.) However, let me say clearly that I do not believe, as astrologers do, that things created by the Creator (like stars) control God's creation (Deuteronomy 18:9–12). However, in the Bible as well as in Bible scholarship (see *The Witness of the Stars*, by E. W. Bullinger, D.D.), Orion is not only considered to be symbolic of a righteous warrior, a savior, and a victor over evil, but it also alludes to the coming victorious Christ, whose very foot stands upon the head of the enemy! *Orion* in ancient Hebrew and Akkadian means "light breaking forth in the Redeemer." In His left hand He holds the head of the "roaring lion" as a token of His victory. For who can stand when He, Jesus, the cosmic Prince of heaven, appears with swift judgment? (See Malachi 3:2; Luke 10:18–19.) This is macro-imagery at its best!

The Original "Star Wars"

Not since the fall of lucifer from heaven has there been a battle like this one. (See Isaiah 14:12–16; Ezekiel 28:14–18; Revelation 12:3–11, 1 Thessalonians 4:16–17.) The most vivid memory I recall of this vision was the fear of God I experienced upon hearing an enormously loud, worldwide, crackling thunder originating from outer space and reverberating throughout the entire earth's atmosphere! Next, I heard a voluminous, corporate groan and shriek from a combined six-and-a-half billion souls crying out simultaneously at the appearance of this great intergalactic explosion (Revelation 1:7). True Christians who loved His appearing were shouting in loud praise and exhilaration, while others cowered in sheer terror and shame at the sight (Zephaniah 2:2). I had the feeling in my stomach of rising upward with my family. It was glorious! The coming of Christ is an incredible, cataclysmic, cosmic event beyond description! Without the aid of television, everyone will easily see the returning Christ, coming with millions and millions of the hosts of heaven. It was a vivid scene spread across the entire solar system—a veritable 360-degree invasion of earth by heaven's inhabitants!

Powers of Ten

String theory has now literally become the "pop physics" of our generation. They state that all the universe is made up of tiny strings of energy. But the fact is, God "holds all of the strings!" In Colossians, Paul taught us that Jesus controls all things in the universe—from the largest spiral galaxies in interstellar space down to the smallest known subatomic particles, such as the tau neutrino. If one looks down he sees eternity. If one looks up he sees eternity! God is omnipotent! I'm glad He's also loving! As Paul taught the church at Colosse, a reflection of the image of Jesus Christ is imprinted upon the physical universe. It's as if God has left His fingerprints on all of creation. Astrophysicists, NASA scientists, space telescopes, and so on, have lately been finding God's fingerprints all over the universe! These fingerprints show incredible cosmological design and

© 2001 Keith Goodson

©2001 Danny Hahlbohm

NO. 15

illustrate clearly that God is a loving, personal Creator. *"Who is the image of the invisible God, the firstborn of every creature: for by him were all things created, that are in heaven, and that are in earth, visible and invisible...All things were created by him, and for him: and he is before all things, and by him all things consist"* (Colossians 1:15–17).

Therefore, I pray that you will ask God to baptize you and fill you with His Holy Spirit. Get oil in your lamps! Trim your lamps! Be filled with the Spirit! (See Matthew 3:11; Luke 11:9–13; Acts 1:8; 2:1–16.)

The Glorified Christ

We will see Him, the Son of God, with eyes as a flame of holy fire, whose body is *"like a jasper...stone"* (Revelation 4:3). He radiates such glory that *"there was under his feet...a sapphire stone"* (Exodus 24:10)! There is a remarkable account in the Bible in which the pre-incarnate Christ physically appears to Moses and the elders of Israel. His glory (His *kabod*) was so powerful, and the weightiness of His presence so awesome that, were it not for His grace, He would have slain the seventy unsanctified elders of Israel.

"And they saw the God of Israel: and there was under his feet as it were a paved work of a sapphire stone, and as it were the body of heaven in his clearness. And upon the nobles of the children of Israel he laid not his hand: also they saw God, and did eat and drink" (Exodus 24:10–11).

According to Old Testament commentators, *Keil-Delitzsch*, the Hebrew meaning of the phrase *"laid not his hand"* connotes "did not harm or destroy." (See Genesis 22:12.) It was a miracle of God's grace that He did not kill the seventy unsanctified, unseparated leaders of Israel. What an awesome sight! The very ground where the pre-incarnate Jesus walked in His glorified body transmitted so much of His glorious fire and holy heat that the kabod crystallized the soil and transformed it into precious sapphire stone! Now it's easy to understand what Peter meant when he said, *"And if the righteous scarcely be saved, where shall the ungodly and the sinner appear [when He returns]?"* (1 Peter 4:18).

A Healthy Fear of the Lord

The "new antinomians" (Latin for antimoral law) preach a form of psychobabble and do not rightly divide the Word of truth. This type of "false liberty" preaching is what the reformation preachers referred to as "a peculiar form of righteousness". John Wesley and other notable revivalists always taught that such "licentious" preaching gave false hope because it always makes the way to heaven much broader than it really is. (Psalm 7:11; Romans 2:9; Matthew 7:14). Wesley preached that God had no special favorites, and that an unregenerated heart had a deceitful nature, by which man always flatters himself and thinks he does well for himself in regard to his own habitual, pet sins—i.e. he is full of his own singular importance. Sadly, such a person can no longer discern that unless there is heartfelt repentance, the wrath of God will abide upon him, and everything he puts his hand to will seem like drudgery!

There is a purifying fear of the Lord that is healthy and liberating to our souls. We need to imbibe of what the Puritans referred to as a God-fearing spirit—the spirit of humility. Humility will cause us to honor and fear God. The fear of the Lord, grounded in humility, is a strong basis for confidence and hope, and a precious inheritance for our children. The fear of the Lord is a fortress, a place of protection, a refuge in the midst of the coming storm. Noah had such a healthy fear. So should we in this day. (See Proverbs 14:26; 1 Peter 1:5.)

"Seek the LORD, all you meek of the earth, who have upheld His justice. Seek righteousness, seek humility. It may be

©2001 Danny Hahlbohm

NO. 8

that you will be hidden in the day of the LORD'S anger" (Zephaniah 2:3 NKJV).

But just imagine, O bride of Christ, you who are listening to this music and reading this little treatise, when He appears, you will be changed into His likeness, and you shall be like Him!

"Beloved, now are we the sons of God, and it doth not yet appear what we shall be: but we know that, when he shall appear, we shall be like him; for we shall see him as he is" (1 John 3:2).

The apostle Paul also said, *"There are also celestial bodies, and bodies terrestrial: but the glory of the celestial is one, and the glory of the terrestrial is another.…Behold, I show you a mystery; we shall not all sleep, but we shall all be changed, in a moment, in the twinkling of an eye, at the last trump: for the trumpet shall sound, and the dead shall be raised incorruptible, and we shall be changed.*

For this corruptible must put on incorruption, and this mortal must put on immortality" (1 Corinthians 15:40, 51–53).

The Celestial City!

We will soon see His beautiful Celestial City, the New Jerusalem, appearing as flawless diamonds, descending from heaven to an earth that has undergone His fiery restitution (2 Peter 3:10–12). The whole creation groans for this moment (Acts 3:21; Romans 8;23; Revelation 21:1–5). In that New Jerusalem, the crystal river, the jeweled mountains, the translucent trees, plants, fruits, and flowers will all have the unique ability to reflect God's glory and light. Nothing in heaven will pridefully attract attention or seek its own glory, but all will reflect His magnificent Shekinah glory and presence.

As in Heaven, So on Earth

Jesus prayed to His Father, *"Thy will be done in earth, as it is in heaven"* (Matthew 6:10). So it should be now in our churches. No individual celebrity or talent, no well-presented sermon or charismatic personality will be able to draw attention to himself in this day. Alas! **True revival is now moving from the platforms to the pews! Our church meetings will become a forum for deep worship, with a subsequent, sovereign move of God's supernatural power, a direct display of His signs and wonders, and His tangible and manifest presence. With His miraculous presence, evangelism becomes a much easier task for us.** The anointing will always break yokes and make our meetings go much more smoothly (Isaiah 10:27). In our evangelistic and church meetings, there must be less of man's presence and more of God's presence. Again, the more the Lord manifests His supernatural presence in our midst, the easier evangelism will become. In

Acts 2, after tongues of fire and a rushing mighty wind fell upon those in the Upper Room, the one hundred and twenty began to speak in heavenly languages. It was not difficult for Peter to witness and bring three thousand into the kingdom in one sermon (Acts 2:1–41).

One Final Word: Prepare Ye!

"For this is he that was spoken of by the prophet [Isaiah], *saying, The voice of one crying in the wilderness, Prepare ye the way of the Lord, Prepare ye the way of the Lord, make his paths straight"* (Matthew 3:3).

If I have one final message to share with you, it is this: Prepare ye! Prepare ye! Prepare ye!

Prepare for what? In the spirit of John the Baptist and Elijah, I say unto you, prepare your hearts in holiness! Seek the Lord while He may be found. Spend time alone with God in prayer, and let Jesus and the Holy Spirit put on you clean, white, holy garments. You can't make yourselves holy or good enough! However, God has given you the precious blood of Jesus, His immutable Word, and His Holy Spirit of grace to prepare your hearts in holiness, in order that you might separate yourselves from this ungodly and perverted generation! Stop copying the world!

Marriage Is Holy to God

Jesus is an eternally faithful Husband to His people. Although many earthly marriages have failed, His faithfulness to His true bride remains forever.

God places great emphasis on the institution of marriage, even if society or a lukewarm church doesn't. The attributes of divine character—such as loyalty, fidelity, faithfulness, unselfishness, integrity, and purity of heart—are just as important to God today as they were in Noah's day.

There is too much divorce, too much of the turning of the head in regard to serious sins, too much adultery, and too much selfishness. God has had enough of it! Judgment is coming to the house of the Lord (1 Peter 4:17)! In a nutshell, there is too much luciferian, self-exalting, "I, me, my" religion in the Western church today masquerading as true Christianity.

Therefore, while there is time, prepare yourselves for the Marriage Supper of the Lamb! Put on clean, white garments! Prepare for the million-year banquet between the bride and the Bridegroom! Prepare to enter His rest beforehand. Stop reading and looking at and imbibing the filthy junk food cooked up in the kitchens of hell! Stop struggling to be holy, and simply begin to pray and read the Word and meditate upon it. Yield to, rest in, and abide in Jesus (John 15:1–5). Then the fruit of the Holy Spirit will flow effortlessly through vital ministries that are not about gimmicks. Such ministries will have powerful, anointed worship in a spirit of holiness and with spiritual depth; they will not seek to emulate ungodly music or wordly entertainment models. They will cast aside carefully contrived programs and slick productions that imitate the world. We need to see a vision of God's living, immu-table glory! We need to meditate upon His Word and see and experience what is to come shortly!

Consider the following prophetic Scriptures. Those who are sincere believers are, one day soon, destined in Christ to see the fulfillment of these Scriptures.

"And immediately I was in the spirit: and, behold, a throne was set in heaven, and one sat on the throne. And he that sat was to look upon like a jasper and a sardine stone: and there was a rainbow round about the throne, in sight like unto an emerald....And out of the throne proceeded lightnings and thunderings and voices: and there were seven lamps of fire burning before the throne, which are the seven Spirits of God. And before the throne there was a sea of glass like unto crystal: and in the midst of the throne, and round about the throne, were four beasts full of eyes before and behind" (Revelation 4:2–3, 5–6).

"And the twelve gates were twelve pearls; every several gate was of one pearl: and the street of the city was pure gold, as it were transparent glass. And I saw no temple therein: for the Lord God Almighty and the Lamb are the temple of it. And the city had no need of the sun, neither of the moon, to shine in it: for the glory of God did lighten it, and the Lamb is the light thereof" (Revelation 21:21–23).

"And he showed me a pure river of water of life, clear as crystal, proceeding out of the throne of God and of the Lamb" (Revelation 22:1).

And I looked, and, behold a whirlwind came out of the north, a great cloud, and a fire infolding itself, and a brightness was about it, and out of the midst thereof as the colour of amber, out of the midst of the fire....As for the likeness of the living creatures, their appearance was like burning coals of fire, and like the appearance of lamps: it went up and down among the living creatures; and the fire was bright, and out of the fire went forth lightning....And above the firmament that was over their heads was the likeness of a throne, as the appearance of a sapphire stone: and upon the likeness of the throne was the likeness as the appearance of a man above upon it. And I saw as the colour of amber, as the appearance of fire round about within it, as the appearance of his loins even upward, and from the appearance of his loins even downward, I saw as it were the appearance of fire, and it had brightness round about. As the appearance of [a rainbow]...so was the appearance of the brightness round about. This was the appearance of the likeness of the glory of the LORD. And when I saw it, I fell upon my face, and I heard a voice of one that spake" (Ezekiel 1:4, 13, 26–28).

As John and Ezekiel fell under the power of God's vision and supernatural presence, and as the weightiness of the supernatural supercedes the weightiness of the natural, so too, we must bow before His presence in awe and wonder. For *"every knee should bow...and...every tongue should confess that Jesus Christ is Lord"* (Philippians 2:10–11). Let us allow His fire to burn out sin, selfishness, vanity, lust, infidelity, adulteries, homosexuality, perversion, uncleanliness, deception, anger, strife, meanness, cruelty, lying, and all the works of the flesh as named by Paul in Galatians 5:19–21.

©2001 Danny Hahlbohm

NO. 18

In addition, the following passages of Scripture are sober warnings from God regarding habitual sins of the body and flesh—things that could disqualify any of us from heaven. Take a close look at 1 Corinthians 6:9–11; Revelation 22:14–15; 21:7–8; Romans 1:24, 27–32; and Jude 18–20.

A Final Prayer

O Lord Jesus, let those who call themselves by Your name repent of anything that would disqualify them from the crown of glory that You have prepared for them from the foundation of the world. You did not come to save us *in* our sins but *from* our sins. We need to know what to repent *from* and what to repent *to*. We know that all the above-mentioned sins of the flesh can easily be overcome as we surrender to and are filled with the Holy Spirit of grace. As He fills us, Your mercy will well up within us and cause us to be what You've called us to be, and will enable us to do what You've called us to do.

Lord Jesus, You are the Lover of my soul! Although You said the way is straight and narrow that leads to eternal life and that few go that way (Matthew 7:14–15), You did not say that it was hard, burdensome, or difficult. Rather, You said that Your yoke is easy and Your burden is light (Matthew 11:28–30; John 10:10). O Lord, we the bride look for Your mercy at Your soon return! O Lord, You will allow no flesh to glory in Your presence. Purify Your people, Your prophets, Your Levitical and prophetic minstrels. Burn out sin, and let Your people reflect Your glory through Your mirror of grace.

"If you love me, keep my commandments" (John 14:15).

Song of Angels® Summary

Glory to God! May the music of this album and the message of this book lift you into new realms of His glory, new realms of the flow of His Spirit. May you feel a fresh touch of His forgiveness, His healing for your soul and body, mind, and spirit (1 Thessalonians 5:23) as you cry out to Him with all your heart (Jeremiah 29:13)! I pray that the words of these songs will stir you to surrender all that you are to Him; to walk in newness of life. I pray that you will not draw back from or fear the "new"; that you will worship in the "new," pray in the "new," and dance in the "new"; that you will see into new realms of the heavenlies; that you will understand the urgency of this hour; that you will be seasoned by fire; and that you will allow Him to transform you into a crystal Christian, transparent and pure and fit to be a habitation of God's divine presence.

Yes, my friend, God is doing a new thing! Rejoice! Lift your hands to heaven and shout!

Glory! Glory! Glory!

Infinite God! My great, unrivaled One!
Whose light eclipses that of yonder sun;
Compared with thine, how dim its
*   beauty seems,*
How quenched the radiance of its golden
*   beams!*

O God! Your creatures, in one strain,
*   agree;—*
All, in all times and places, speak of thee
Even I, with trembling heart and
*   stammering tongue*
Attempt thy praise, and join the general
*   song…*

There is light in yonder skies,
A light unseen by outward eyes;—
But clear and bright to inward sense,

It shines, the star of Providence.

The radiance of the central throne,
It comes from God, and God alone;
The ray that never yet grew pale,
The star that shines within the veil.

And faith, unchecked by earthly fears,
Shall light its eye, though filled with tears,
And while around 'tis dark as night,
Untired, shall mark that heavenly light.

In vain they smite me. Men but do
What God permits with different view;
To outward sight they wield the rod,
But faith proclaims it all of God.
Unmoved, then, let me keep thy way,
Supported by that cheering ray,
Which, shining distant, renders clear
The clouds and darkness thronging near…

Peace has unveiled her smiling face,
And woos thy soul to her embrace;
Enjoyed with ease, if thou refrain
From selfish love, else sought in vain;

She dwells with all who truth prefer,
But seeks not them who seek not her.

Yield to the Lord with simple heart,
All that thou hast, and all thou art;
Renounce all strength but strength Divine,
And peace shall be fore ever thine;
Behold the path which I have trod—
My path till I go home to God!"*

Come on! There's victory in the blood of Jesus! God the Father, God the Son, and God the Holy Spirit love you, and so do I! You are more than a conqueror through Him who loves you! Surrender to His grace! Become a soldier in the battle for righteousness and truth, and walk in victory! The angels and the heavenly hosts are watching while they prepare for you your heavenly abode and your triumphant entry into heaven. And yes, all the while they sing the *Song of Angels*®.

Burdened for souls

and aflame in His love,

Freddy Hayler
(Ephesians 3:20–21)

Excerpts from "God's Glory and Goodness," "The Light above Us," and "The Entire Surrender" by Madame Jeanne Guyon

A Personal Testimony from Freddy Hayler

On a more personal note, I would like share with you some spiritual insights and experiences that my wife and I have had regarding heavenly visions and encounters with the Lord Jesus and His angels. In fact, our testimonies are the theme in which the lyrics of the entire *Song of Angels®* is based. If God could save a soul like mine, He can save anyone!

Early On

I was born into a Catholic, Bostonian family of ten children. Although I had some general religious convictions, I had no genuine faith in Christ. I just had nominal faith in God and did not really understand what it meant, in the biblical sense, to be born again and baptized in the Holy Spirit until I was twenty years old. However, I had my first supernatural encounter with God while barely a teenager. On a warm summer Fourth of July night, I was nearly dying from a drug overdose. It was in that desperate overdose situation and struggle for life that Jesus first appeared to me in a vision. I was virtually dying. He literally restarted my heart and taught me how to "breathe again." I know this might sound strange to some who have never been involved with heavy drugs and gangs, but due to the effects of the drug overdose, my bodily functions literally began to stop. It was at that moment, when Jesus rescued me from certain death and asphyxiation, that I first realized that He is a personal God of love who intensely cared whether I lived or not. It was as if, centuries earlier, Ezekiel had seen me in my own sorry plight when he made the following prophecy regarding the mercy of God on sinners:

"None eye pitied thee, to do any of these unto thee, to have compassion upon thee; but thou was cast out in the open field, to the loathing of thy person, in the day that thou was born. And when I passed by thee, and saw thee polluted in thine own blood, I said unto thee when thou was in thy blood, Live; yea, I said unto thee when thou was in thy blood, Live" (Ezekiel 16:5–6).

When I was a very young teenager, I was lying not just in an open field, but on a major interstate highway at 2:00 A.M., not knowing where I was or the fact that cars were speeding by me at seventy miles per hour!

Several years passed after that experience. Though I had quit drugs; attended Saint John's Prep, a Catholic preparatory school administered by some wonderful Xavian and Franciscan brothers; and improved in my "good works" and fear of God, I still did not have a personal experience of the saving grace of the Lord in my life. Maybe God was allowing certain things to happen in my life for a purpose, but I just didn't know *how* to experience Him. (See Romans 8:28.) In fact, little did I know at the time that I was about to be birthed into the kingdom of God by another supernatural encounter with Jesus!

As college student, on the evening before Good Friday, and while I was under the weight of sin and deep depression, I had a supernatural encounter with the God of all life. Directly after a Fellowship of Christian Athletes meeting on campus, I was challenged by the coach of the football team to consider the declarations of the risen Christ and to receive Him as Lord and Savior. Later that same evening, a brother led me in the sinner's prayer to be born again, and I experienced something that would change my life forever. For the first time in my life, I experienced the living God. Only then did I begin to fully understand Scriptures that I had read in a gospel tract several years earlier. I promised the Lord that if I ever had the privilege of producing my own album, I would always present His eternal plan of redemption for those who would listen to it. I wish I had heard such a plan earlier in my own life.

For you who are non-believers in Christ, I pray that, as you listen to this music and read this book, you will begin your journey to eternity at the foot of the cross of Calvary. This is the place of God's sacrifice, and this is the place where your "old man" must die in order for your "new man" to be born again (Romans 6:6; Ephesians 4:22–24; Colossians 3:9–10). This is where Jesus was crucified and where His blood was poured out for the for-giveness of your sins. God wants you to become a new creature in Christ (2 Corinthians 5:17). There is no substance in the universe more powerful than the royal, red, ruby blood of the Lord Jesus Christ that will cleanse you from all your sins. Repent, therefore. Turn from your sins and ask Him to cleanse you of all your sins of omission and commission (known and unknown). And you know what? Jesus will do it.

The simple tract I found contained the following Scriptures. You who do not know Christ, confess and memorize these Scriptures.

God's Simple Plan of Salvation

Jesus desires to come into your heart right now. Today is the day of salvation (2 Corinthians 6:2). All you have to do is ask Jesus to come into your heart, and confess and believe in these Scriptures:

© 2001 Thomas Blackshear II

NO. 24

JESUS...
THE BAPTIZER IN FIRE

[Matthew 3:11]

"For all have sinned, and come short of the glory of God" (Romans 3:23).

For the wages of sin is death; but the gift of God is eternal life through Jesus Christ our Lord" (Romans 6:23).

"For God so loved the world, that he gave His only begotten Son, whosoever believeth in him should not perish, but have everlasting life" (John 3:16).

"Marvel not that I said unto thee, Ye must be born again" (John 3:7).

"Behold, I stand at the door, and knock: if any man hear my voice, and open the door, I will come in to him, and will sup with him, and he with me" (Revelation 3:20).

"That if thou shalt confess with thy mouth the Lord Jesus, and shalt believe in thine heart that God hath raised him from the dead, thou shalt be saved. For with the heart man believeth unto righteousness; and with the mouth confession is made unto salvation" (Romans 10:9–10).

The Next Step

After receiving Christ as Lord and Savior, I naturally wanted all that Jesus offered to me in the Bible! I wanted to be empowered for holy living and effective ministry. So should you.

As a young Catholic I had heard of the baptism of the Holy Spirit. I had heard this mentioned in a ceremony called "Confirmation," but I didn't realize that the third person of the Trinity wanted to fill me and live through me. (See John 14:12–18; 15:26; 16:7–14.) Later in my walk with God, I discovered in my studies of past revivals that many of the great evangelists and Christian statesmen (John Wesley, Charles Finney, D. L. Moody, R. A. Torrey, Evan Roberts,

Andrew Murray, Watchman Nee, and so on) all had experienced what they called a "second work of grace," a "baptism of fire," or the baptism of the Holy Spirit. As I repented of my sins and asked Jesus into my heart and for Him to baptize me in the Holy Spirit, I felt unutterable words of love and fire well up from my stomach (John 7:38). I then began to utter what Paul referred to in the Scriptures as a heavenly language.

"With groanings which cannot be uttered" (Romans 8:26).

> **"Groanings which cannot be uttered are often prayers which cannot be refused."**
> **—Charles H. Spurgeon**

It was as if a bolt of white-hot lightning struck me on the top of my head and ran through my entire body. I began to leap for joy and went running to and fro on the campus, proclaiming, "Jesus is alive! Jesus is alive!" Hundreds of students studying in their dorms for finals had their windows open that balmy spring night, and undoubtedly they heard the plan of salvation shouted from the famed Sunken Gardens in historic Williamsburg, Virginia! Quite frankly, I did not care what any person thought of me. Like the unconverted pseudo-educated Saul of Tarsus, I had become a fool for Jesus! (See Romans 1:16; 1 Corinthians 4:10.) I really wanted to be filled with the Holy Spirit and would not let the fear of the unknown rob me from God's great gift of the Holy Spirit. Later that evening, I rushed back to my dorm room like a Berean Christian to search the Scriptures for a validation of my biblical experience. I say as St. Augustine did, "I do not understand in order to believe, but I believe in order that I might understand."

Faith in God will always precede true knowledge of Him.

Now faith is the substance of things hoped for, the evidence of things not seen....But without faith it is impossible to please him: for he that cometh to God must believe that he is, and that he is a rewarder of them that diligently seek him" (Hebrews 11:1, 6).

"Without faith it is impossible to please him!" Don't even think of approaching God without it! In fact, God wants you to have a supernatural encounter of a heavenly kind! But *you* must seek, *you* must find, and *you* must do it as a little child by faith alone. Ask and you will receive; seek and you will find.

"If ye then, being evil, know how to give good gifts unto your children: how much more shall your heavenly Father give the Holy Spirit to them that ask him?" (Luke 11:13).

"There are different kinds of fire; there is false fire. No one knows us better than we do, but we are not such fools as to refuse good bank notes because there are false ones in circulation; and although we see here and there manifestations of what appears to us to be nothing more than merely earthly fire, we nonetheless prize and value and seek for the genuine fire which comes fresh from the altar of the Lord."

—William Booth

"Don't come to me with your rubbish, that there is no emotion in religion. You cannot have real religion without emotion. There never has been a revival without emotion, and there never will."

—Donald Gee

Fire on You Again!

"And, being assembled together with them, commanded them that they should not depart from Jerusalem, but wait for the promise of the Father, which, saith he, ye have heard of me. For John truly baptized with water; but ye shall be baptized with the Holy

Ghost not many days hence...But ye shall receive power, after that the Holy Ghost is come upon you: and ye shall be witnesses unto me both in Jerusalem, and in all Judea, and in Samaria, and unto the uttermost parts of the earth" (Acts 1:4–5, 8).

And when the day of Pentecost was fully come they were all with one accord in one place. And suddenly there came a sound from heaven as of a rushing mighty wind, and it filled all the house where they were sitting. And there appeared unto them cloven tongues like as of fire, and it sat upon each of them. And they were all filled with the Holy Ghost, and began to speak with other tongues, as the Spirit gave them utterance (Acts 2:1–4).

"Now when the apostles which were at Jerusalem heard that Samaria had received the word of God, thy sent unto them Peter and John: who, when they were come down, prayed for them, that they might receive the Holy Ghost: (for as yet he was fallen upon none of them: only they were baptized in the name of the Lord Jesus.) Then laid they their hands on them, and they received the Holy Ghost" (Acts 8:14–17).

"While Peter yet spoke these words, the Holy Ghost fell on all them which heard the word. And they of the circumcision which believed were astonished, as many as came with Peter, because that on the Gentiles also was poured out the gift of the Holy Ghost. For they heard them speak with tongues, and magnify God. Then answered Peter, Can any man forbid water, that these should not be baptized, which have received the Holy Ghost as well as we?" (Acts 10:44–47).

"He said unto them, Have ye received the Holy Ghost since ye believed?...Then said Paul, John verily baptized with the baptism of repentance....When they heard this, they were baptized in the *name of the Lord Jesus. And when Paul had laid his hands upon them, the Holy Ghost came on them; and they spake with tongues, and prophesied"* (Acts 19:2, 4–6).

It is evident from the context that it was a habit of Paul to ask believers this question when he met them: "Have you received the Holy Spirit since you believed?" It is plain here that the apostle, upon meeting these certain believers, had no idea that they were the disciples of John the Baptist until *after* he asked them this question. It is appropriate, therefore, that we should ask other believers in this day, "Have you received the Holy Spirit since you believed?"

Jesus admonished His disciples who walked with Him on earth for nearly three years to receive the Holy Spirit that He would send them upon His return to His heavenly Father (John 20:22). He knew that they would need the dynamite power of the baptism of the Holy Spirit in order to overcome the spirit of darkness in the world and the bondage of satan's supernatural power. That is why He told them to wait in Jerusalem and seek earnestly this great blessing before evangelizing the world. So we should do the same (Acts 1:4–8).

The prophet Isaiah wrote centuries earlier of a generation of believers who would yield their tongues to the Holy Spirit: *"For with stammering lips and another tongue will he speak to this people"* (Isaiah 28:11)

"Likewise, the Spirit also helpeth our infirmities: for we know not what we should pray for as we ought: but the Spirit itself maketh intercession for us with groanings which cannot be uttered" (Romans 8:26).

NO. 14

The apostle Paul said that it is God's desire to baptize ("immerse," in Greek) you in water, but the Bible figuratively speaks of other baptisms, as well. In Hebrews 6:2, the Bible speaks of the *doctrine of baptisms* ("immersions"). In one sense, there is only *one* baptism into Christ. This occurs at the moment we ask Jesus to come into our hearts in order to be born again. There is a passing of the old nature and a birth of the new. (See Romans 6:3; 10:9,10; 1 Corinthians 12:13; 2 Corinthians 5:17–21.) This is a spiritual phenomena that occurs when the Spirit of God literally thrusts us into the spiritual body of our Lord and Savior. His life is now our life, and we live by faith in the Son of God (Galatians 2:20–21). But before this can occur, the Bible speaks of a baptism of repentance. We see this in the ministry of John the Baptist (see Mark 1:4; Luke 3:3), and also strongly evidenced in Peter's preaching.

"Then Peter said unto them, Repent, and be baptized every one of you in the name of Jesus Christ for the remission of sins, and ye shall receive the gift of the Holy Ghost" (Acts 2:38).

The early church, in fact, preached that the fullness of the Holy Spirit was to be preceded by repentance and confession in Christ. In other words, early Christians were taught by church fathers to fully receive the Holy Spirit at conversion. Yet many today fail to teach unbelievers that one needs to ask Jesus into his heart first in order to be filled with the Holy Spirit. They teach that with simple confession, the new convert "gets it all," but as Catherine Marshall has written, there is indeed "something more." John Wesley called this "something more" a "second work of grace" (or entire santification), while D. L. Moody called it the baptism of the Holy Spirit. Therefore, before we can come to Christ, we must ask God to immerse us in a spirit of repentance from the sins of the Adamic nature and dead religious works. We then take the next step to publically proclaim what has already occurred in our hearts through faith in Jesus (Mark 16:16).

We today, like the early church, need to reestablish the fact that there are other *immersions* that are extremely important to us as believers. Yes, there is a baptism into water (an outward act of obedience to God's commands), but there also needs to be an understanding concerning the baptism into the blood of Jesus, the baptism into His Holy Spirit, and the baptism of fire!

The Sprinkling of His Blood

Jesus is our Passover Lamb, and without the shedding of blood there is no remission of sins. (See Exodus 12:3–7; Leviticus 17:6–12; Luke 22:44; John 6:48–58; 1 Corinthians 5:7; 11:23–29; Hebrews 9:22; 10:21–22; 12:24; 1 Peter 2:24; Revelation 12:10–11.) The sacrament of Holy Communion, or the Lord's Supper, is an outward celebration of believers to remember the shedding of His precious, all-powerful blood for the forgiveness of sins and for our healing. Upon our sincere, first confession of Jesus Christ as Lord and Savior, the Holy Spirit performs a mystical baptism that the eye cannot see (John 3:8). The apostle Peter spoke of the Holy Spirit sprinkling the blood of Jesus upon our consciences (1 Peter 1:2). This is a supernatural baptism or sprinkling that we cannot see with our natural eyes, although we feel the power of it working in our lives through faith when we confess Christ as Lord and Savior. The baptism of blood involves the Holy Spirit, who is the Baptizer; and the medium is the blood of Jesus, whose blood now and forever has been offered upon the mercy seat in heaven (Hebrews 9:12–25).

Baptism into Christ's Death

However, in Romans 6:3–6, Paul also spoke of a baptism of death. Watchman Nee has written a wonderful book entitled *The Normal Christian Life*. It speaks of a baptism into Christ's death (Romans 6:1–10; Colossians 2:12). As we begin to walk with God, we see that we need to continually consider ourselves as dead to the old sin nature. We need to daily consider ourselves dead with Christ (Galatians 2:20). The baptism of death is an ongoing crucifying of the old sin nature by seeing ourselves as vicariously crucified with Christ. We need this daily reckoning in order to conquer the sins that would so easily beset us (Romans 6:1–6).

Baptism in Water

There is also a baptism in water, in which man is the *baptizer* and the medium is *water* (H_2O). The water is an outward sign and witness, to men and to God, that the person being baptized is confirming his or her inward experience of salvation (John 3:10–17) and is willing to identify with the substitutionary death of Christ on the cross. By the outward act of obedience in submitting oneself to going down into the waters (with the aid of a person in ministry), one symbolizes his burial with Christ. As he comes up out of the water, this typifies his new, resurrected life in Jesus!

Baptism of Fire

But there is another baptism that many Christians still need to experience. Yes, at salvation, you obtain the Father, the Son, and the Holy Spirit (Matthew 28:19). In fact, all three dwell in you by God's grace, through simple, sincere faith in Jesus Christ! You cannot divide the Trinity. But there is something more that the Bible speaks of after salvation, and it's for every believer! Let me give you a simple illustration. When you have a guest visit you at your home and you are not at the front door to greet him, you may call out from the kitchen or from another room, "Come on in; I'll be with you in a minute." As the person stands in the foyer, he or she is in fact waiting to be received. The guest is in the house, but because that guest has manners, he will not just walk in and make himself at home. You must first leave the kitchen and go and receive your guest in order for him to make himself at home. So it is with the person of the Holy Spirit. At salvation, He is like a guest coming into our home (our temple, which is our spirit, soul, and body). We must then fully receive Him in order to make our whole home entirely His (1 Thessalonians 5:23; 1 Corinthians 6:19)! Therefore, as believers, we should now want to receive the Holy Spirit and ask Him to fill and inhabit our whole house. This is what John the Baptist spoke of when he said, "*I indeed baptize you with water unto repentance: but he that cometh after me is mightier than I, whose shoes I am not worthy to bear: he shall baptize you with the Holy Ghost, and with fire*" (Matthew 3:11).

Jesus also said, "*If ye then, being evil, know how to give good gifts unto your children: how much more shall your heavenly Father give the Holy Spirit to them that ask him?*" (Luke 11:13).

Here we see that the baptism of the Holy Spirit involves Jesus as the Baptizer, and the "medium" is not a medium at all but the third person of the Trinity—the fiery Holy Spirit of God! I ask, therefore, how can one be baptized in fire if that individual does

©2001 Keith Goodson

NO. 22

NO. 11b

not know Jesus to begin with? How can you ask someone whom you do not know to do something? Some may say, "But I got the Holy Spirit at salvation!" This is true; you do have the Holy Spirit. Certainly the baptism of the Holy Spirit can occur simultaneously with one's conversion. The Bible records this occurrence (Acts 2:38). But receiving Him is a different experience altogether.

We also find that the baptism in the Holy Spirit can precede water baptism. Water baptism is an important part of our obedience and sanctification, but it is not a prerequisite for salvation (Acts 10:47–48). But many Christians have not because they ask not, or they have not because they do not know to ask.

> "How little chance the Holy Ghost has nowadays. The churches have so bound Him in red tape that they practically ask Him to sit in a corner while they do the work themselves."
> —C. T. Studd

The Holy Spirit is a gentleman. He has manners. He will never force Himself upon anyone. He will only fill and immerse a pure vessel who has been washed in the blood of Jesus—a vessel who is consecrated, set apart, and hungry for more of Him. He patiently waits for you to ask Him to fill your life! But first there must be thirst. There must be hunger. All of us as believers should ask Jesus to completely fill us with the Holy Spirit! This empowers one for service. This is what the disciples waited for in the Upper Room (Acts 1:8; 2:1–10). We need all of God's baptisms (immersions) in order to avail ourselves of the full measure of the fruit of the Spirit (Galatians 5:22–23) and the supernatural gifts of the Spirit. The apostle Paul taught us to seek "continual infillings" of the Holy Spirit. One of the ways to stay filled with the Holy Spirit is found in the following passage.

"And be not drunk with wine, wherein is excess, but be filled [in Greek this signifies a continual filling] with the Spirit; speaking to yourselves in psalms and hymns and spiritual songs, singing and making melody in your heart to the Lord" (Ephesians 5:18–19).

You cannot be filled with the Holy Spirit if you are living in habitual and unrepentant sin, because the pure Spirit of God is holy. The Holy Spirit can be grieved, quenched, insulted, withdrawn, and even—God forbid— deliberately blasphemed (Mark 3:22–30; Galatians 5:22–24).

"Who is he that overcometh the world, but he that believeth that Jesus is the Son of God? This is he that came by water and blood, even Jesus Christ; not by water only, but by water and blood. It is the Spirit that beareth witness, because the Spirit is truth….And there are three that bear witness in earth, the Spirit, and the water, and the blood: and these three agree in one" (1 John 5:5–6, 8).

In other words, the entire Trinity is involved with our salvation. Again, you cannot separate the Godhead!

Yes, you do get the Holy Spirit at salvation. He comes into your heart. But now you need to ask the Lord to take you to the next level. You need to get in an upper room and ask for the Holy Spirit to fall upon you, fill you, and immerse your entire being in order to have increased effectiveness in Christian ministry. Otherwise, you are not operating on all cylinders! The one hundred and twenty people of the inner circle of Jesus were hungry enough to pray and seek God's face for ten straight days before the Holy Spirit came upon them mightily in the Upper Room (Acts 2:1–4). Therefore, ask the Lord Jesus, whom you now know and love through your salvation experience, to baptize you in the fire of His Holy Spirit, even as John Wesley, Charles Finney, D. L. Moody, R. A. Torrey, Andrew Murray, Watchman Nee, and many other great saints throughout the ages have experienced.

The Holy Spirit: Don't Leave Home without Him

Therefore, if you want to flow in the supernatural and walk in victory and holiness during this evil hour, you need the baptism in the Holy Spirit! Having this wonderful experience will lead to your operating more and more in the gifts of the Holy Spirit and will cause you to continually walk in the Holy Spirit's infillings. Your entire ministry will have increased spiritual fruit beyond what you can imagine possible (1 Corinthians 12–14; Ephesians 3:20–21).

Decently and in Order

It is decent and in order for churches today to pray for the sick, cast out devils, praise and dance before the Lord, and so on.

These are the acts of the "new creature" (Matthew 10:8; Mark 16:17–18). It is intriguing to study the apostle Paul's explanation to the church of Corinth regarding the spiritual gifts God has promised to all His people who desire them. The Corinthians were misusing the gifts (1 Corinthians 14:1). Paul commanded all of us, regardless of our denominational background, to earnestly desire the spiritual gifts of the Holy Spirit (1 Corinthians 12–14). Some of these gifts are revelatory; some are power gifts; but whether the greatest or the least, why would any Christian not desire *all* of them? The Apostle Paul differentiates between the *private* and *public* use of tongues. According to Jude verse 20, we are admonished to pray in the Spirit always. The Apostle Paul, ("…I speak in tongues more than any of you!") in no way diminishes the private use of tongues for personal and spiritual edification. When he says "tongues is the least of the gifts" he is referring to its order in the public assembly.

Regarding the gift of tongues Paul said, *"He that speaketh in an unknown tongue edifieth himself....For if I pray in an unknown tongue, my spirit prayeth, but my understanding is unfruitful"* (1 Corinthians 14:4, 14).

I cannot conclude from the plain meaning of the text and the original Greek language, even for a moment, how some Bible teachers intimate that tongues (*glossolalia* in Greek) mean learned human languages (1 Corinthians 13:1)!

Regarding the other supernatural gifts Paul said, *"To another faith by the same Spirit; to another the gifts of healing by the same Spirit; to another the working of miracles; to another prophecy; to another discerning of spirits; to another divers kinds of tongues; to another the interpretation of tongues: but all these worketh that one and the selfsame Spirit, dividing to every man severally as he will"* (1 Corinthians 12:9–11).

At the time of my salvation, I had no understanding of the above Scriptures, which I later realized confirmed what was happening to me experientially! It didn't matter what people thought of me; I was going to be a witness for Jesus after experiencing the God of my salvation! God had healed my mind and delivered me from the guilt of sin and inner fear. Many were converted that following year on that campus.

Paul wrote to Timothy, *"For God hath not given us the spirit of fear; but of power, and of love, and of a sound mind"* (2 Timothy 1:7). I must have confessed that Scripture promise thousands of times during that summer as God did a tremendous work of inner healing in my life. Listen, my friend. God will do the same for you if you cry out to Him with all your heart. It doesn't matter what situation you're in. It doesn't matter how far you have backslidden, or whether you are in bondage to drugs, alcohol, or sins of immorality. It doesn't matter if your mind has since been burned out by sinful abuse, what sin you've committed, what you've done, or whatever the devil has done to you. "*God is no respecter of persons*" (Acts 10:34). What He has done for me He will do for you! He is the great Deliverer, Healer, Savior, and Redeemer! (See Acts 4:12; 10:34, 38.)

Celestial Encounters with God

In fact, this album and this book are about supernatural encounters with God, to which you and I are entitled as believers. The real, "normal" Christian life involves the supernatural power of God. It is abnormal for the evangelical church to primarily operate in the cerebral realm, or the lower realm of the emotions, when God wants our spirit-man to come alive. (1 Thessalonians 5:23). Even some Pentecostal movements can become traditionalized. The church today generally operates too much in the human intellect. There-fore, we need to stay away from men's traditions, which are void of the glory of God.

Whether we're involved in high church liturgy or charismatic enthusiasm, let us examine our hearts to see if we are truly seeking God's living presence and holiness of character (1 Corinthians 11:28; 2 Corinthians 13:5).

And let us not just always look for the "lightning-bolt" experience, because God can visit us in a variety of ways that oftentimes are simply gentle impressions by the wooing of the Holy Spirit's still, small voice. It has been said that the Lord will *whisper* to you through His Word in Bible study, *speak* to you through your conscience and through the God-given authorities in your life, and *shout* to you through your trials and tribulations! However, we still should also consider that if the Lord would operate with supernatural and tangible power and miracles in the early church, why would we expect Him to move differently in the present church age (Hebrews 13:8)? Has God changed His ways just because we have the complete New Testament revelation? Let us never forget there is no "Amen" at the end of the book of Acts! This is because the supernatural acts of the Holy Spirit continue until this day. I can say from firsthand experience that God's miraculous power and His holy angels have not deserted us for another universe!

A *Divine Sense of Urgency*

It is now time for Christian households to sanctify their homes of evil things and influences. We need to keep our children from the knowledge of evil and the unholy anti-law spirit of new antinomianism that pervades our churches and culture. As in Noah's day, God is still more concerned about the qualitative conditions of our hearts rather than the boasts of spurious, false conversions. We need to "*chanak*" (Hebrew, Strongs #H2596); that is, we as parents are to narrow our children's exposure to and understanding of evil. That may mean no "spending the night" with certain individuals, or strictly controlling what your children see on television (including ungodly, demonic commercials)! (See Romans 16:19.) "*Train* [chanak] *up a child in the way he should go: and when he is old, he will not depart from it*" (Proverbs 22:6).

It has been my prayer that, in some profoundly small and simple way, this music and this message will encourage you to love Jesus more than ever before. Dear church, please welcome the precious Holy Spirit. Let us not through sin or unbelief grieve or quench Him any longer! We should pray, "Holy Spirit, please come!" Indeed, the anointing of the Holy Spirit has been likened to oil throughout the Bible. As satan's time-lease on planet Earth is expiring, he has stepped up his spiritual warfare against the saints. That's why Jesus admonished us to keep oil in our lamps, for without the fullness of the precious Holy Spirit, it will be hard to stand in these troubling times. Therefore, like a good soldier, stand, my brother and sister. The time is short! Prepare your hearts in purity and holiness! Get oil in your lamps! Jesus is coming! Maranantha!

Tons of love!

Freddy and Annie Hayler

2001 Song of Angels® Project, Volume 1

About Archangels and the Living Creatures

The study of angels is in fact an inquiry into another aspect of the glory of God's presence in the world.

"But though we, or an angel from heaven, preach any other gospel unto you than that which we have preached unto you, let him be accursed" (Galatians 1:8).

The purpose of the study of angels should lead true Christians to fear God and to glorify the Lord Jesus Christ, who created them in order to carry out His redemptive plan of salvation (Hebrews 1:7, 14). Paul admonished us not to worship angels or to be overly fixated by their presence like some in the New Age movement. (See Colossians 2:18; Galatians 1:12; 2 Thessalonians 2:9–11.)

However, after one encounters such a creature, one is awed beyond imagination at the power and glory of God. Below is a list of some of the more well-known, angelic generals of heaven.

• **Gabriel** (in Hebrew, "strong man of God"): he is a messenger archangel who reveals future events, and gives understanding to eschatological visions and wisdom to those he informs. In Luke 1:11–20, he appeared to announce the birth of Jesus the Messiah. His instrument will be the trumpet sound heard at the coming of our Lord Jesus Christ at the end of this age (1 Thessalonians 4:16).

• **Michael** (in Hebrew, "who is like God?"): a general among the celestial archangels, a heavenly prince, and a patron angel of Israel, he champions God's people over the fallen archangel lucifer (Daniel 12:1). He is a heavenly prince who stands up and intercedes for the saints of God. (See Daniel 10:13, 20). In the final battle he will lead the celestial hosts of heaven to battle against and destroy the forces of lucifer and hell (Revelation 12:7).

In almost all ancient Jewish literature,[2] Michael is the vindicator of Israel against Edom, Sodom, and all the wicked forces of hell. He is also the head administrator of the heavenly records, the chief librarian who is in charge of recording all the thoughts, words, and actions of every soul sent into the world by God Almighty (Acts 7:38). He was an intermediary between God and Moses. In Jude 9, he disputed over the body of Moses with satan.

Extrabiblical Angelic Encounters throughout Church History

There is no Scripture that emphatically states that Michael is the only archangel, even though he is the only angel referred to as such. Many Bible scholars believe that Gabriel is an archangel, as well. Other archangels not mentioned in the Bible, but mentioned throughout ancient church history, are discussed below. Keep in mind that the following angelic names, even though they are not found in the Bible, have been an important part of Jewish and early church history and are nonetheless very fascinating characters to consider.

• **Ariel** (in Hebrew, as taken from Genesis 46:16 and Numbers 26:17, means "Lion of El," that is, "Lion of God"): according to Jewish scholars and Jewish prophetic literature, Ariel is also a cryptic name for Jerusalem. (See Isaiah 29:7, 12 and endnote 2.)

In Israeli cryptic literature, Ariel is considered to be one of the major arch-angels of God, along with Michael, Uriel, Gabriel, Metatron, and others. He is also considered to be the fierce defender of Jerusalem and a patron archangel of Israel who will destroy any enemy with the fire of God's wrath.

In Jewish intertestamental literature, Ariel is described as a heavenly luminary, a powerful archangel of Yahweh who jealously protects the Holy City. All that come against that city will be destroyed with his fiery sword.

• **Raphael** (in Hebrew, "angel of healing" or "the healing blessing"): he was seen in numerous visions of the ancient Jewish prophets as recorded in Jewish intertestamental literature. In Enoch 20:23 of the Apocrypha, he was sent by God to remove a disease from the eyes of Tobit, a holy Jewish leader. He is very active in human affairs on planet Earth; he is a power-

ful, cosmic prince imbued with the compassion of God and sent by God to stir the healing waters.

Could this be the patron angel noted in the Bible at the pool of Bethesda (John 5:2–6)? Only the Lord knows for sure, but it is an interesting thought.

• **Uriel** (in Hebrew, "flame of God"): in Jewish prophecy and history, he is ranked with the other chief archangels such as Michael, Gabriel, and Raphael. He serves as God's messenger and as a guide to visions of God. He is a mighty general of heaven.

• **Metatron** (in Hebrew, "angel of countenance," because he witnesses at all times the countenance of the holy Father): Jewish scholars call this mighty archangel by the name of Metatron. He works with God and for God in order to extend God's plan to those who are heirs of salvation.[3]

The Zoe

The Ophanim are mentioned in the Old Testament pseudopigrapha documents of ancient Jewish prophets. Ophanim are a class of holy, living, celestial creatures—inhabitants of the throne of God—also known as the zoe creatures (Revelation 4:5–7).

Opanni'el YHWH is of the ophanim class of celestial creatures, according to ancient visionaries. In Jewish intertestamental literature, they are described as mind-boggling, awesome creatures, having sixteen faces, four faces on each side, and one hundred wings on each side. They also have 2,191 eyes on each side, making a total of 8,766 eyes (which corresponds with the number of hours in a year). From each pair of eyes in each of the faces, lightnings flash forth. From every eye, torches blaze. No human form could ever look upon such a creature without being consumed instantly, and no human genius or great imagination then or now could ever imagine its indescribable appearance and existence. According to ancient Jewish scholars, the prophet Enoch wrote that it would take twenty-five hundred years to traverse its length by foot, and no one can calculate the amplitude of its power or its strength except God, the King of Kings, Himself.

The prophet Enoch also stated that the Opanni'el arranges the runnings of the fiery wheels of the other living creatures. It tends to and beautifies the living creatures and arranges their platforms, adorns their compartments, and makes their turnings smooth to increase their function and beauty. Thus, the Ophanni'el magnify and reflect the glory of the Creator's majesty and make others swift to

NO. 9

incessantly praise the Creator God.

According to the Bible, similar creatures are described as being full of eyes and full of wings (Revelation 4:5–7). According to the Jewish scholars who recorded these extrabiblical accounts, each zoe creatire had seventy-two large sapphire stones set in its garments, with four large emeralds set in each crown. Their countenances were as brilliant as the sun, and they dwelled in unapproachable pavilions of splendor and light. The brilliance of the Shekinah was upon them; the splendor of God's glory was upon their faces. Sapphire stones encircled them, with pillars of fire flanking them. Thus, with the Opanni'el, the celestial mega-creature's main function is to glorify God, protect God's throne, and beautify the living creatures of the ophanim-zoe class (Revelation 4:6).

The ancient prophet Enoch described one of these angelic creatures as being over two hundred thousand miles tall! This seems to correlate with the magnitude of angels described in Revelation (Revelation 10:1–5; 14:19; 16:8; 18:1–3; 19:1). Angels are not all overly effeminate, wimpy-looking creatures or infantile, fat, little cherubs as historically portrayed by so many artists. However, the prophet Zechariah saw two angels who definitely appeared as "women with wings".[Zech. 5:9]

The Holy "Watcher" Angels

Above these creatures and directly opposite the Most Holy One's throne are what the ancient prophets of Israel referred to as the "watchers of the divine presence." These are the highest, noblest, most honored, fearsome, beloved, wonderful angels. They are greater than all other celestial luminaries created by God. Among all the ministers of heaven, none is equal to them. Their abode is directly opposite the throne of God's glory. Their station is facing the Holy One, blessed be He, so that the splendor, light rays, and beams of God's reflected glory resemble and mirror God's own splendor—the brilliance of their image nearing but never equaling the brilliance of the Shekinah. Ancient scholars wrote that God has delegated through them the execution of His divine justice. In other words, they will judge and abase the arrogant and prideful rebellious ones of the earth. Each of the watcher angels' names is written with a pen of flame upon each of their crowns. Sparks and lightnings stream out from them. A river of holy fire flows among them and ignites the stones of fire that blaze around God Almighty's holy presence. Myriads of angels bathe in the holy fire in order to constantly beautify and purify their garments. Some of these holy creatures are larger in size than the planet Earth. How marvelous and awesome is our God! What awesome and dreadful visions did these ancient Jewish prophets have![4]

In summary, we as Christian believers know that God and His Son, Jesus Christ, are the primary focus of our interest, study, worship, and adoration. We know that all of heaven's translucent beings are created in order to reflect His glory. We know that the Lord Jesus Christ is our sole King of Kings, Lord of Lords, Savior, and Healer. Yet it is still edifying and comforting to know that in both testaments of the Bible, along with Jewish scholarship and prophecy, there are plenteous accounts of visions and tangible experiences that heirs of salvation have had with these extraterrestrial, celestial beings that are delegated by God to help those true believers who are the heirs of salvation (Hebrews 1:14). Although it is

encouraging to know all this about angels, we are warned by Paul never to worship or focus on the creation more than the Creator (Romans 1:25).

Yes, as with the elect today, men and women of God in ancient times who were consecrated and who sought God in prayer were rewarded with blessed visions of angelic beings and heavenly vistas of the throne. We should be grateful they have left for Jewish and Christian posterity their ethereal impressions.

I therefore leave you not only with the lyrics and music of the vision that the Lord has given me, but also with several quotes of more recent prophets of God.

> "Angels...have a greater influence on this world than men are generally aware of. We ought to admire the grace of God toward us sinful creatures in that He has appointed His holy angels to guard us against mischiefs of wicked spirits who are always intending our hurt both to our bodies and to our souls."
> —Increase Mather

"Angels where'r we go,
Attend our steps whate'r betide,
With watchful care their charge attend,
And evil turn aside."
—Rev. Charles Wesley

"White and dazzling…every angel was surrounded with an aura of rainbows so brilliant, that, were it not withheld, no human being could stand the sight of it."
—William Booth

To conclude, I pray that all of us who are hungering for God's presence in this hour, who desire to be a vital part of God's end-times reformation army, will get a supernatural revelation of the grandeur and greatness of God and will see more clearly that the real purpose of the *Song of Angels*® is the exaltation of the glorious, risen Jesus Christ. I prayer that, after considering the subjects and spiritual truths mentioned in this little book, we will all become more effective in praising Him and in lifting Him up, so that all men indeed will be drawn to Him. May the end-times revival to which God is calling increase, and may all of us be found faithfully working in His final harvest fields, so that when He comes He may say to us, "Well done, good and faithful servant of the Lord!" Glory be to God!

"And I, if I be lifted up from the earth, will draw all men unto me" (John 12:32).

endnote 1: *God's Simple Plan of Salvation*, ©1991 Robert Ford Porter. Used by permission.

endnote 2: To quote from Dr. J. A. Charlesworth, professor of New Testament Literature, "These lost sources would be extensive; it would include at least the following: the Book of the Wars of Yahweh (Numbers 21:14), the Book of the Just (Joshua 10:13; 2 Samuel 1:18), the Book of the Acts of Solomon (1 Kings 11:41), the Book of the Annals of the Kings of Israel (1 Kings 14:19; 2 Chronicles 33:18; 2 Chronicles 20:34), the Book of the Annals of the Kings of Judah (1 Kings 14:29; 15:7), the Annals of Samuel the Seer (1 Chronicles 29:29), the History of Nathan the Prophet (2 Chronicles 9:29), the Annals of Shemaiah the Prophet and of Iddo the Seer (2 Chronicles 12:15), the Annals of Jehu, Son of Hanani (2 Chronicles 20:34), an unknown and untitled writing of Isaiah (2 Chronicles 26:22), and an unknown lament for Josiah by Jeremiah (2 Chronicles 35:25).

endnote 3: From *Angels*, by Dr. Billy Graham (Word Publishing).

endnote 4: From the Old Testament pseudepigrapha documents of ancient Jewish prophets, volumes 1 and 2; apocalyptic literature and testaments, edited by James H. Charlesworth. Some translations taken from "The Testament of Solomon" (Oxford University Press).

Bloch

Plate D

Thank Yous

I would first like to give praise, glory, honor, and thanks to God the Father, to the Lord Jesus Christ, my precious Savior, and to the Holy Spirit, who inspired the message of this album and book. I would also like to thank my God-fearing, lovely wife, Annie, whose constant love, unshakable faith, and intercessions constantly challenge me to go deeper with God. I thank my two lovely daughters, Lindsay and Rebekah, for their love and encouragement and musical contributions to the project.

Thanks also to my teacher and spiritual father from Israel—a leader of leaders—God's general, Dr. Costa Salim Deir (and his wonderful wife, Ruth). The apostle Paul said, *"You have not many fathers"* (1 Corinthians 4:15). Therefore, I would like to thank another father in the faith, Dr. David Minor and his precious wife, Lorraine, for their prayers and their prophetic input into our lives and ministry.

Thanks to Christy and Betty Wilson (powerful missionaries to Afghanistan), my spiritual advisors at Gordon-Conwell Seminary, and to Dr. Peter Wagner at Fuller Theological Seminary Center for Church Growth. Many thanks to Dr. Ralph Winter, U.S. Center for World Missions, along with Don Richardson—devout missionaries to the unreached ("ta ethne") people groups of the planet—for giving me a passion for souls and to reach the nations in order to fulfill Matthew 24:14. To Dick Reuben, shalom and thanks for the spiritual insights. Thanks to South African evangelists Warren and Kayla Hunter, whose zeal and deep understanding of the supernatural realm have caused to us go deeper still into the realms of God's glory; to brother Tommy Tenney, whose suggestions and anointed books have blessed me beyond measure; to Ruth Heflin, whose anointed ministry and books also have made a deep impact on my music and ministry; to evangelist Steve Hill, who prophesied and imparted vision and anointing into my life and Annie's; to Pastors John and Anne Gimenez, whom I first met in 1975, and who married Anne and me—our friends for life!

To those who helped make this project a reality—thanks to Kit and Debbie Austin, Denny and Ellen Anderson. To Jerome and Lucia Hines, for your friendship, prayers, and vocal training; to John Nathan at Sugar-Melodi U.S.A. and Gruppo Editoriale Sugar, Milan, Italy (Sugar Music Group - Italy), the most beautiful music in the world! Bella Musica! Manifico! Gloria! Thanks to Golden Altar Records for believing in the vision and having integrity and loyalty to see it through so that its message can be communicated globally. To Anne's Mom and Dad in Orlando, who helped inspire me to sing; and to my mother, my four brothers and five sisters and their loving families; and to my extended family in Boston, Massachusetts, and Providence, Rhode Island—love and thanks to all of you!

As with the fiery seraphim and archangels above, let us all be consumed with a holy, burning love for Jesus, and be aflame with an ardent passion to reach souls for Christ. The time is short!

Your brother in Christ,

Freddy "Frederico" Hayler
Ephesians 3:20–21

Producer: Freddy "Frederico" Hayler
Executive Producer: Anne Hayler
**Soundtrack and Musical Arrangement/
Transcription Production:** Freddy Hayler and
Steve Errante
Conceptual Design, Writing, and Editing:
Anne and Freddy Hayler
Sound Engineers and Computer Programming: J.
K. Loftin, C. F. Studios, Wilmington, NC

Recorded and realized with 24-bit technology at Crystal
Sea Studios, Hampstead, NC; Quad Studios, Nashville,
TN; and C. F. Studios, Wilmington, NC

Mastering: Masterphonics, Nashville, TN

Musicians:
Piano: Rolin Mains
Lead Guitar: Paul Brannon
Oboe and English Horn: Bobby Taylor
Clarinet: Lee Levine
Cello Solo:
French Horn: Jennifer Kummer
Pedal Steel Guitar: Clyde Mattocks
Strings: David Davidson and the Nashville String Machine
Keyboards and Synthesizer: John Devries
Female Soloist: Rebekah Hayler
Photography: Brownie Harris, New York, and
Wilmington, NC; Marshall Marvelli, Winston
Salem, NC

CD and Front Cover Art:
conceptual by Freddy Hayler, Golden Altar Records
Design: Ford Design Group, LLC

Computer and Website Design: Jerome Belton
Publishing:
Track 10: Insieme S.r.l./Zucchero & Fornaciari
Track 5: Insieme S.r.l./Sugar Music Ed. Musicali S.r.l.
Track 4: Ed. BMG Ariola Spa/Assist S.r.l.
Tracks 1, 2, 3, 8, 13, 14: Sugar-Melodi, Inc.,
  Edizioni Suvini Zerboni Spa/Sugar Music
  Edizioni S.r.l./Mascotte; Track 9 Insieme S.r.l.
Tracks 11, 12: Walton Music Corporation, ASCAP
Track 7: Warner/Chappell Music Publishing

**Personal Management and International
Representation:** Anne Hayler
Tel: (910) 270-3242 in the United States
Fax: (910) 270-3240

Official Website: www.songofangels.com

Mailing Address:
Golden Altar Recordings
P.O. Box 10740
Wilmington, NC 28404 USA
Tel: (910) 270-3242
E-mail: declaringHim@cs.com

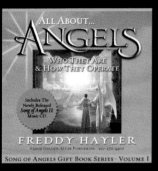
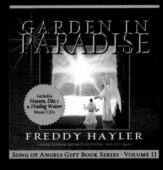

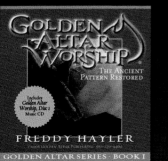
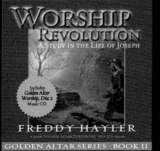
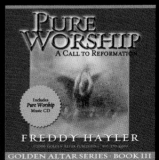

Personal Notes

_____

_____

_____

_____

_____

_____

_____

_____

_____

_____

_____

_____

_____

This book of the law shall not depart out of thy mouth; but thou shalt meditate therein day and night, that thou mayest observe to do according to all that is written therin: for then thou shalt make thy way prosperous, and then thou shalt have good success.
—Joshua 1:8

Personal Notes

_____

_____

_____

_____

_____

_____

_____

_____

_____

_____

_____

_____

_____

_____

Thy word have I hid in mine heart, that I might not sin against thee.
—Psalm 119:11

ALSO AVAILABLE

Song of Angels® CD
ISBN/SPCN: 555-423-1756
UPC: 809-037-700-125

The timeless, ethereal music of *Song of Angels*® declares the glory of the Lord Jesus Christ in a language of global music that all of the nations of the world can understand. Let the dynamic, anointed voice of Freddy Hayler and the new sounds of the Celestial Symphony Orchestra take you into a place in the Spirit, a new dimensional realm of the heavenlies, and on into His glorious presence! All glory to the Lord as we worship with the *Song of Angels*®!

How Great Thou Art CD
ISBN/SPCN: 076-011-0468
UPC: 083-061-010-225

Coming soon:
Freddy Hayler with the
London Symphony Orchestra

Healing Wateres Worship
The Glory of Christmas
Hymns of Glory
Sacred Classics

For more information on Freddy "Frederico" Hayler's future releases,
send e-mail to: declaringHim@cs.com.

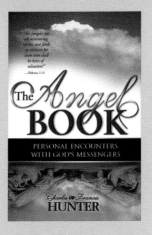

The Angel Book
Charles & Frances Hunter
ISBN: 0-88368-598-1 • Trade • 216 pages

Charles and Frances Hunter describe their own
personal encounters with angels and what the Bible
tells us about these messengers of God. They report
on the different kinds of angels and their roles,
how God's messengers can impact your life, and
how to experience the presence of God. God uses
angels to protect us, comfort and encourage, bring
strength during trials, help us witness to others,
wage spiritual warfare, communicate His will to us,
and bring answers to prayer. The Bible records over
one hundred appearances of angels to both men
and women. Discover the many purposes of angels,
both historically and in your daily life.

WHITAKER
HOUSE

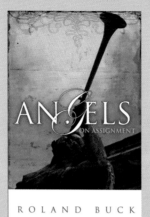

Angels on Assignment

Roland Buck

ISBN: 0-88368-697-X • Trade • 192 pages

In this intriguing book, Roland Buck describes his
personal encounters with angels and what the Bible
tells us about these messengers of God. You'll find
out how God's messengers impact your own life
and how God is using angels to help usher in the
great end-times harvest of souls before the return
of Jesus. As you become aware of the remarkable
role of these messengers of God, you'll gain
increased faith and confidence in God's plan for
your life, for the ministry of believers, and for the
salvation of multitudes of people leading to the
second coming of Christ.

Angels to Help You
Lester Sumrall
ISBN: 0-88368-564-7 • Digest • 128 pages

Angels not only played an important role in
biblical history, but they continue to intervene in
people's lives today. Lester Sumrall offers scriptural
answers to many often-asked questions about
angels, such as, "How can I personally be aided by
angels?" and "How did angels help Jesus during His
time on earth?" You might not realize it, but your
life is strongly influenced by angels. Find out how
in this helpful, easy-to-read guide. During a time of
much misinformation about angelic activities, this
book offers the truth about angels.

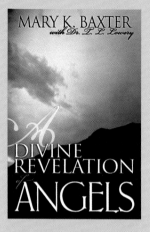

A Divine Revelation of Angels
Mary K. Baxter with T. L. Lowery
ISBN: 0-88368-866-2 • Digest • 288 pages

Best-selling author Mary Baxter describes dreams, visions, and revelations of angels that God has given her. Explore the fascinating dynamics of angelic beings—their appearance, their assigned functions and roles, and how they operate, not only in the heavenly realms, but also in our lives here on earth. God's holy angels are magnificent beings who are His messengers and warriors sent to assist, sustain, protect, and deliver us through the power of Christ.

WHITAKER HOUSE